Fort Phantom Hill

Fort Phantom Hill

The Mysterious Ruins on the
Clear Fork of the Brazos River

Bill Wright

State◆House
Press
Buffalo Gap, Texas

Library of Congress Cataloging-in-Publication Data

Wright , Bill
Fort Phantom Hill: The Mysterious Ruins on the Clear Fork of the Brazos River
Bill Wright
  p. cm.
Includes Bibliographical references and index.
ISBN- 978-1-933337-58-6 (pbk. alk. paper)
ISBN- 933337-58-3 (pbk. alk. paper)
ISBN- 978-1-933337-55-5 (cloth: alk.paper)
1. History United States/Civil War Period (1850-1877) 2. . 3. United States: History-19th century.
This paper meets the requirements of ANSI/NISO, Z39.48-1992 (permanence of paper)
Binding materials have been chosen for durability ∞
I. Title.
          "Cataloging-in-Publication Data available from the Library of Congress"

Manufactured in the United States
Copyright 2013, State House Press
All Rights Reserved
First Edition

State House Press
P.O. Box 818
Buffalo Gap, Texas 79508
325-572-3974 · 325-572-3991 (fax)
www.tfhcc.com

Printed in the United States of America
Distributed by Texas A&M University Press Consortium
800-826-8911
www.tamupress.com

ISBN-13: 978-1-933337-58-6
ISBN-10: 1-933337-58-3

Book Design by Rosenbohm Graphic Design

Contents

Images past to present of Fort Phantom Hill on pages 71 to 81.

Acknowledgments

Having lived in Abilene, Texas, most of my life, I have always been aware of the lonely chimneys of Fort Phantom Hill in neighboring Jones County. They have given many visitors silent testimony to the travails of settlers when our area was on the very western frontier of Texas. Writing this book has been a pleasure because it has afforded me a much broader knowledge of the events leading up to the establishment of the fort, details of its mission and abandonment, and the many uses the location has subsequently served. Of course, such as task is never a solo task. There have been many contributors to the effort. Foremost is, of course, Alice, my wife who has endured my frustrations with research and organization and who has supported my work in many other ways. My assistants over the years, Beverly Guthrie, Angie Cook, Kim Edwards, and most recently, Kelly Craig, have been invaluable.

I have sought advice from many including Robert Pace, Ph.D., ex-Chairman of the History Department at McMurry University, Stephen L. Hardin, Ph.D., also of the History Department at McMurry University, Dedie Taylor, historian, editor, and scholar, and Mary Lee Bartlett, Ph.D. Archaeologist.

I appreciate the critical review and careful editing of the manuscript by Dr. Robert Sledge, retired professor of history at McMurry University and the thoughtful preparation of the manuscript by Claudia Gravier Frigo, project manager.

I couldn't have completed this project without the aid of my research assistant, Amanda Jones. Amanda has tracked this project from beginning to completion, obtaining permissions and confirming citations. The research librarians at the Center for American History at the University of Texas, Katherine Best and Matt Darby, guided me through the extensive manuscript collection at that institution, and Evelyn Lemons, Fort Concho National Historic Site, and Mary Williams, archivist and historian at Fort Davis National Monument, provided valuable material. Shea Woodard, Staff Assistant for Senator Kay Bailey Hutchison, helped with photograph acquisition.

Princess among the historians whose work I depended upon was Martha Doty Freeman, whose exhaustive research for the Fort Phantom Foundation provided a well-documented framework for my own work. She is a magnificent and meticulous researcher who knows most of the archives dealing with the subject and whose comprehensive bibliography covered almost every aspect of

ACKNOWLEDGMENTS

Fort Phantom Hill and other frontier forts of the era. I appreciate also H. Allen Anderson of Texas Tech University whose narrative history of Fort Phantom Hill in the 1976 West Texas Museum Association Yearbook pulled much of the story together. Of course, I also owe a debt of gratitude to all historians, past and present, who have published work relating to Fort Phantom Hill. I have special debts to Donald S. Frazier, Ph.D. of the McWhiney History Education Group and McMurry University whose extraordinary class on writing history helped me complete the manuscript, and Jim Alexander, who guided me among the ruins and whose foresight has preserved them for future generations. I deeply appreciate the corrections to the manuscript suggested by my erudite friend, Erik Mason, whose awesome knowledge of history, the English language, and military procedure informs his essential advice. Marcia Hatfield Daudistel read the manuscript and made some helpful suggestions.

To all of these and others, I am grateful. Any errors or omissions in this work are my responsibility alone and do not reflect on those whose work I relied upon or who assisted me with this project.

Bill Wright
Abilene, Texas
2013

Introduction

The prairie flowers were blooming in 1881 when Mary Clack, along with her husband, John, suggested to several of their Abilene friends that they go fishing in the Clear Fork River in nearby Jones County. They also planned to visit friends who had moved there some time before. The standing chimneys of old Fort Phantom Hill were a short distance from the river, and Mary's friends had promised her a trip through the ruins before they returned to their new home in Abilene.

Earlier that year, on March 15th, the Texas & Pacific railroad held a lot sale, establishing the town that had steadily grown as the railroad's traffic increased, and more settlers sought cheap land in the unsettled western plains of Texas.

John B. Clack, anticipating the sale of lots by the railroad, had purchased land south of the future town on Lytle Creek the year before. John also saw the country the winter before, traveling from his home in Tarrant County to hunt buffalo, and discovered the high grassland of Taylor County could be a place for him to settle permanently. With his brother, Mack, and three others, they brought their young families to the open range of Taylor County and established a home.

John's wife, Mary was a teenager when their prairie schooner made the trip west from the more settled eastern part of Texas. Soon, the Clack family established friendships in the community, where the isolation of the new railroad town drew everyone closer together in the frontier spirit. Fishing trips to the Clear Fork were one of the few opportunities for entertainment afforded them.

On this particular day, the women soon grew tired of fishing and walked along the river, collecting the abundant wildflowers and enjoying the cool breeze as it blew up from the river, rustling the leaves and grasses with their white seed heads. They wondered about the fort. What had life been like for the soldiers stationed

1

there? What battles had they fought? How had it been decided to place it here, on this gentle slope with the grass stretching to the horizon? As the sun finally sank below the prairie's edge, and anticipating supper of fried fresh catfish caught by their husbands, they decided they would accept their host's invitation to take a tour of the ruins in the morning.

After breakfast in their friend's home, they crossed the river and walked to the fort. As the name suggested, they thought that indeed, the low hill seemed like a phantom hill with stark chimneys rising from ground. Mary's first sight of at the ruins stirred her emotions. "It is here that I pause for lack of words to convey the impression of the mind when the sight of that old ruined fortress burst upon my view," she wrote. "The numerous chimneys each standing alone, like sentinels guarding the ruins of a wall now gone; the heaps of stones scattered about these excavations telling a story that will live after those who occupied them are forgotten except among the heroes of Texas history, and then even the half will remain untold."[1]

Mary was impressed that the chimneys had survived the extremes of heat and cold, the winds and rains of the harsh west Texas weather, and still stood "erect as if defying the enemy."[2] She remarked that the soldiers seemed to have destroyed the logs used for the walls when they left, presumably to keep them from being used by the Indians and that latecomers had salvaged stone and wood for new construction elsewhere.

In her book, Mary observed that she saw what seemed to be "embankments" connecting the various buildings and wondered about their use, thinking perhaps they were dirt piles from tunnels that once connected the various facilities, enabling men to move between them unobserved.[3]

She commented on the stone corral that had contained the horses and the old "arsenal" where the ammunition was kept. It was the only building with a remaining roof.

Around the buildings, were the remains of a stockade or other type of fortification. The posts were gone but visible mounds of dirt were indications of where they had been placed.

Mary concluded her observations with perhaps the first call for the preservation of the fort. She asked:

> [W]hy tear it down! Why destroy that which would mean so much to posterity. Instead of unthoughtedly destroying the place that shielded

our men while fighting to make the West a safe place for us to live, why not preserve that which is left of it, and then use those scattered stones in erecting a monument to the memory of those heroes who gave up freedom, home and in many instances, life for the welfare of this same posterity. Let this monument extend high above all other buildings standing about the place, and l[e]t the names of every soldier who was stationed here be carved on the sides, together with a brief history telling the world what it was all about.[4]

* * *

Today, passers-by ask themselves the same questions: what must it have been like in the early days when the fort had been staffed with soldiers? In 1851, when the fort was established overlooking the now friendly hills and river bottoms, Indians threatened not only the soldiers but also the settled areas far to the east that the fort was constructed to defend. What a flimsy line of defense the fort appeared to be!

Throughout history, walls and lines of defense have both separated and detained human populations. Walls defended the earliest community of Jericho, and the Roman emperor Hadrian's occupation of Britain. Walls, both physical and political, have attempted to control both the movements of peoples and the spread of ideas.

The history of Fort Phantom Hill is an interesting saga of defense, a story of both political necessity and individual hubris, and a tale of human perseverance and shortsightedness. The story of the "Post on the Brazos River" has all the elements that characterize human activity with its triumphs and tragedies, victories and defeats.

Visions of America's Manifest Destiny, and the inexorable tide of immigration into newly occupied but unsettled lands, created a need for protection of the visionary newcomers. Conflicts in Texas with the government of Mexico and the resulting war of independence, statehood, yet another war with Mexico, and a Civil War produced turmoil and uncertainty. As time passed, circumstances dictated changing uses for the structures at Fort Phantom Hill, from military outpost to stage station to hunter's outpost. Eventually, opportunities for adaptation ran their course and the stone structures fell into neglect. The frontier was occupied by new immigrants who possessed a more modern technology. The threat of Indians was replaced by the hard daily work of living in a semi-desert environment.

By weaving the threads of this story into the larger warp and weft of western history, one begins to understand how this small fort was conceived, lived, and died as an important part of the "winning of the West."

Visions of Manifest Destiny

In 1846, at the beginning of the Mexican War, Alexander William Doniphan became colonel of the First Missouri Mounted Regiment and led an expedition to Santa Fe to support Stephen W. Kearney during the battle for northern Mexico, now New Mexico. A member of the expedition, Private John T. Hughes, a former schoolteacher, recorded in his memoirs an encounter with a party of traders who were returning from Santa Fe to Independence, Missouri.

It was a beautiful spring day, but a time burdened with the tensions between the United States and Mexico that led to war over the annexation of Texas. Hughes noted that a late afternoon thunderstorm broke, drenching the travelers, but refreshing the air. When it passed, and as twilight approached the Great Plains, the men looked at the storm clouds as they passed across the sinking sun and were amazed to see them form the image of an eagle. Hughes said they cried out with one voice that it was a sign of events to come. Soon, they believed, the "eagle of liberty" would "spread its broad pinions over the plains of the west and the flag of our country would wave over the cities of New Mexico and Chihuahua."[1]

War, like a thunderstorm, would bring a freshening of the course of empire. Such was the temperament of the young nation: here was a vast wilderness to be occupied with lands for all and unbridled opportunity. A half-century of exploration—starting with British adventurer Alexander Mackenzie in 1793 followed by the rival expedition of Lewis and Clark in 1804—had revealed the

George Caleb Bingham, *Daniel Boone Escorting Settlers through the Cumberland Gap*, 1851–52. Oil on canvas, 36 1/2 × 50 1/4. Mildred Lane Kemper Art Museum, Washington University in St. Louis. Gift of Nathaniel Phillips, 1890.

extent of the lands beyond the eastern ribbon of settlement. The national appetite was whetted. The 1845 annexation of Texas by the United States stoked the fires of what journalist John L. O'Sullivan termed "Manifest Destiny." Now, men like Doniphan, Hughes, and their companions became bearers of this dream: The United States, extending from coast to coast, a vision soon realized with the subsequent war with Mexico.

Nor were Hughes and his comrades alone in their determination to expand the national horizons. Popular expressions of this mood soon emerged, including epic art. George Caleb Bingham depicted the nation's expansionist past with his 1852 *Daniel Boone Escorting Settlers through the Cumberland Gap*; German landscape master artist Emanuel Gottlieb Leutze cast his *Westward the Course of Empire Takes Its Way* a decade later, whereas Painter John Gast, whose painting *American Progress* depicted Colombia leading the settlers onward while Indians and animals scattered before her, created his painting nearly three decades after Hughes made his journey.

All these men, inspired as they were by the spirit of American destiny, simply followed in the footsteps of a generation of countrymen who traditionally had economic motives in their push westward. The allure of cheap land in the former

Westward the Course of Empire Takes Its Way by Emanuel Gottlieb Leutze. Courtesy of Architect of the Capitol.

Mexican territory of Texas had drawn entrepreneurs of all stripes: adventurers, thieves, and homesteaders. When American settlers first built their log cabins along the banks of the Brazos in 1823, there were only about three thousand Spanish-speaking Tejanos in the province. In 1830 there were an estimated fifteen thousand people in Texas, still a part of Mexico, but now overwhelmingly English-speaking. In just twenty years, shortly after the annexation by the United States in 1845 that sparked war with Mexico—and had drawn Hughes onto the Great Plains, the population had exploded to 212,592, including 58,161 slaves.[2]

These slaves stood in the path of Manifest Destiny. Texas, settled mostly by Southerners, embraced forced servitude and that fact made slavery an obstacle in the political process of annexation. The free states were determined to limit the addition of slave-holding states, but the Southern states were anxious to increase the number for both practical and political reasons. In the end, the imperative of Manifest Destiny overcame the economic, moral, and political wranglings surrounding slavery[3] and allowed the addition of the territory to the United States.

Many of the Texians, as these Anglo settlers of Mexican Tejas called themselves, hoped that annexation to the United States would bring with it the protection of the state's borders by the federal government. They were equally concerned for defense from the native tribes who were seeing their land appropriated by the

American Progress by John Gast. Courtesy of the Autry National Center, Los Angeles: 92.126.1.

increasing number of immigrants. Further, there was also an economic benefit. As greater security became a reality, more immigrants would feel free to come to Texas, increasing profits for the Texian property owners.

The first test of this faith in the protecting aegis of the United States came in the Mexican War. The hostility between the United States and Mexico finally reached a tipping point on April 25, 1846, when an American patrol encountered two thousand Mexican troops encamped at a hacienda near present Brownsville. A battle ensued and the outnumbered Americans were captured and imprisoned in Matamoros. A few days later on May 3, Mexican artillery under the command of General Pedro de Ampudia and General Francisco Mejia began firing on Fort Texas located north of the Rio Grande in present-day Brownsville, Texas.[4] While this was occurring, General Zachary Taylor engaged Mexican forces at Palo Alto and Resaca de la Palma. On May 8, 1846, President James K. Polk declared war on Mexico, ostensibly to protect and preserve its newly acquired territory. The resulting war preserved not only the lands of the former republic of Texas but it also added vast areas, including California to the United States, completing the connection between the oceans and fulfilling the spirit of Manifest Destiny. The United States now stretched from sea to sea.

2

Exploring the Western Territory

The War with Mexico ended with the 1848 Treaty of Guadalupe Hidalgo, which, along with other provisions, required the federal government to protect populations on both sides of the Mexican border from raids by Texas Indians. Additionally, because the frontier was also a flashpoint for scofflaws of many kinds, the government was obligated to protect the Indians as well.[1] This protection was especially important because the end of the conflict spurred a substantial increase of immigration to Texas.

Land was filed for and new counties organized in the frontier regions, some consolidated with those areas already occupied. Because the early Texas immigrants were concentrated along the eastern Texas border, the southern coast of the Gulf of Mexico, and the Rio Grande Valley, many of the newcomers eyed the unsettled lands even further west. The federal government took action to control and manage these new territories acquired from Mexico.

It was necessary to survey the new boundary between the two countries and plan for the extension of railroads connecting the United States and its new territories as well as providing for the influx of immigrants. To accomplish this, roads were necessary.[2] However, the great expanse of western Texas between the

Three Comanche Indians. Courtesy of the library of Congress online photographic archives, Photo #3b01742u.

eastern and southern part of the state and the Spanish-colonized El Paso del Norte (modern-day Ciudad Juárez) was not hospitable to transients and discouraged permanent settlement. An area known as the Cross Timbers, a band of Post and Blackjack oak unfit for timber, growing in coarse sandy soil, extended from central Oklahoma and into central Texas, bisecting the northern and central portions of the state. West of this area and beyond the grasslands that formed the southern extent of the Great Plains, the character of the land changed to desert shrub where water was scarce and known springs and other resources undependable. It was a *despoblado*, or wasteland: a vast prairie land of low rainfall, rolling plains, and seasonal streams with a scattered and mostly transient Indian population, all of which presented substantial obstacles to travel.

Despite obstacles, more and more settlers left the more populated areas and came to the frontier. They found that the character of the land and the climate were not the only obstacles they would face because these western lands were not unoccupied; they would have to deal with Indians.

Great
Chihuahuan Desert

Charles D.Grear

The earlier Paleo-Indians, known mostly from their flint artifacts, had hunted the area for thousands of years. Following them, later arrivals, the Comanche, Wichita, Apache, and other groups of nomadic Indians, traveled these plains. The Indian tribes moved with the seasons and the bison, competing with each other for territory.

Indians thought about land differently than the white settlers. Ownership was not a concept they embraced. Land was simply there and they used it. Even before the Europeans discovered this new land, the various Indian tribes competed vigorously with each other for the use of desirable territory. It was not the peaceful Eden some would have us believe. This freedom to roam the open spaces following the immense herds of buffalo on their annual migrations was central to their survival as well as their culture. Naturally, the incursions of the European immigrants attempting to control the territory as their own created new conflicts. The newcomers, like any other conquering group, were equally robust in

11

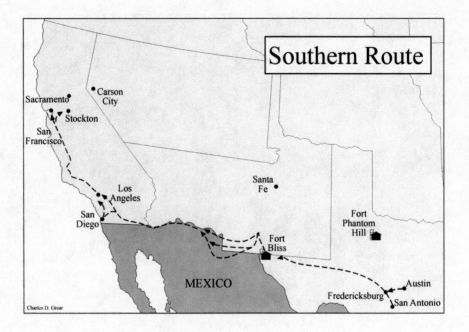

attempting to secure this new domain as their own. As historian Rupert Richardson observed, "the people of Texas loved peace, but they loved land more."[3]

Magnifying the problem for the resident Indians in 1848 was the discovery of gold in California, which soon had hopefuls swarming westward to find riches. For decades, Americans reached the Pacific by routes across the middle Great Plains. These wilderness roads and trails had to negotiate treacherous stretches through the Rocky Mountains where problems were created not only by the difficult landscape, but also by the severe winter weather. To counter these challenges many began to consider a route that carried them across the west Texas plains where travel appeared less problematic.

Even so, this warmer and more level course was not necessarily easier. Along this route not only were the immigrants in constant danger from Indians, but they also faced lack of water in the northern expanses of the great Chihuahuan Desert that lay astride their path.[4]

The availability of water was the most important item in determining the routes. In the beginning, the migrants generally followed established trails traversing the Indian country, creating minimal disturbance to the native population. Even then, because the Indians depended on the same sources of water, their travel and hunting tactics were disrupted.

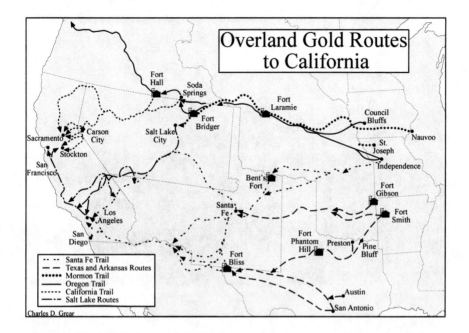

Many migrants followed the popular Santa Fe Trail, which began in Old Franklin, Missouri, traversing Indian lands westward to Santa Fe. As word continued to spread about the possibility of great riches in California, the rush for gold overwhelmed the established trails and many travelers simply set out across the uncharted land on their own. Then, in 1859 when gold was discovered in Colorado, William Bent (who with his brother Charles, operated a trading post on the Santa Fe Trail from 1833 to 1849) estimated sixty thousand people crossed the plains in that year alone.

Others came through Texas. They followed a southern route that had several branches, one of which followed trails from San Antonio and Austin, through Fredericksburg and westward to the Pecos crossings and El Paso. From this former Spanish outpost, they continued toward California by a variety of routes, dipping southward into Mexico for some, whereas others chose the "Sonora Route" following Civil War hero and military explorer Colonel Philip St. George Cooke's wagon trail, probably joining it near present Garfield, New Mexico, then crossing the Animas Mountains and through the Guadalupe Pass on the border of Mexico. They followed the Santa Cruz River to the presidio of Tucson, crossing the formidable Sonoran desert across the Gila country in southwestern Arizona and then, on to California.[5]

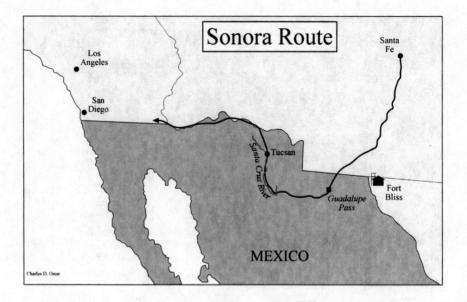

Another branch of the southern route through Texas generally followed the trail established by Captain Randolph B. Marcy in 1849.[6] This route went through Buffalo Springs, southeast of present-day Wichita Falls. Buffalo Springs became a favorite camping ground for travelers to the gold fields. Leaving there, the route continued west through Olney, Rotan, and Big Spring toward the Horsehead Crossing of the Pecos before joining the main southern route through Fort Davis to El Paso.

Although this branch was not the most popular route west, it still formed the basis for the later road traveled by the Butterfield Overland mail and, still later, portions of a transcontinental railroad. The southern route was somewhat longer than those through the mid-continent but the weather was better and the Indian problem less severe.

In addition to the need for roads as settlers and gold seekers moved west in 1849, the military recognized that manpower at the existing forts would be inadequate to defend the frontier. The sudden annexation of the vast western territories plus the discovery of gold in Sutter's Mill in California had launched one of the largest land migrations in history. Even the Indians, who were aware that the eastern tribes had been overrun by Europeans, still could not imagine what was to come and were certain to resist the newcomers as the eastern tribes did. In 1846, Army Lieutenant J. W. Albert interviewed a Cheyenne Chief, Yellowknife, at Brent's Fort, Colorado. In his journal he wrote:

> [Yellowknife] . . . is a man of considerable influence, of enlarged views, and gifted with more foresight than any other man in his tribe. He frequently talks of the diminishing numbers of his people, and the decrease of the once abundant buffalo. He says that in a few more years they will become extinct; and unless the Indians wish to pass away also, they will have to adopt the habits of the white people, using such measures to produce subsistence as will render them independent of the precarious reliance afforded by the game.[7]

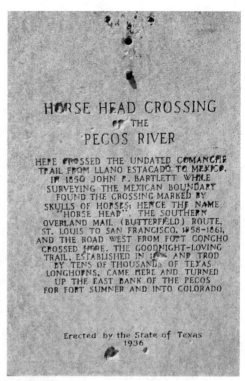

HORSE HEAD CROSSING
of THE
PECOS RIVER

HERE CROSSED THE UNDATED COMANCHE
TRAIL FROM LLANO ESTACADO TO MEXICO.
IN 1850 JOHN R. BARTLETT WHILE
SURVEYING THE MEXICAN BOUNDARY
FOUND THE CROSSING MARKED BY
SKULLS OF HORSES; HENCE THE NAME
"HORSE HEAD". THE SOUTHERN
OVERLAND MAIL (BUTTERFIELD) ROUTE,
ST. LOUIS TO SAN FRANCISCO, 1858-1861,
AND THE ROAD WEST FROM FORT CONCHO
CROSSED HERE. THE GOODNIGHT-LOVING
TRAIL, ESTABLISHED IN 1866 AND TROD
BY TENS OF THOUSANDS OF TEXAS
LONGHORNS, CAME HERE AND TURNED
UP THE EAST BANK OF THE PECOS
FOR FORT SUMNER AND INTO COLORADO

Erected by the State of Texas
1936

Horsehead Crossing. Courtesy of Bill Wright, author.

As Yellowknife anticipated, many of the tribes west of the Mississippi opposed the transients and homesteaders trespassing on their historic lands rather than adopting their ways. The Army, tasked with the responsibility of protecting the immigrants who settled or passed through Texas, realized that roads were needed for protection of the immigrants and homesteaders, as well as opportunities for commerce that the new territories presented. To aid development, the federal government developed a program consisting of three parts. First was a commitment to open the western territories to settlement and commerce. Second was the government's recognition of the need for transcontinental railroads linking the new territories with the settled areas of the eastern United States; surveys would determine the most efficient routes. Finally, there was the need to survey the southwestern area, especially along the new border with Mexico.

Because Texas shared a long border with Mexico and contained within its borders a large number of potentially hostile Indians roaming a large and mostly

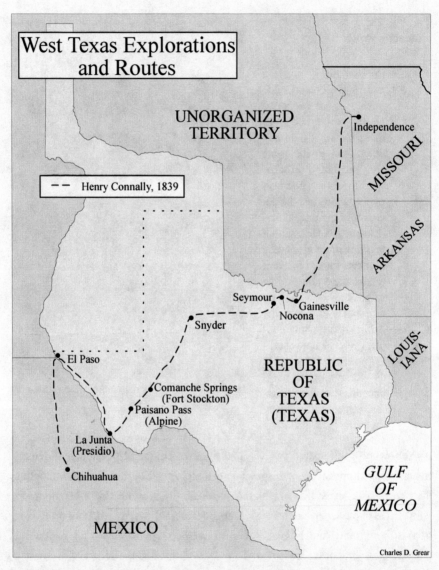

West Texas Explorations and Routes

UNORGANIZED TERRITORY

Independence

MISSOURI

ARKANSAS

– – Henry Connally, 1839

Seymour
Gainesville
Nocona

Snyder

El Paso

LOUIS-IANA

REPUBLIC
OF
TEXAS
(TEXAS)

Comanche Springs
(Fort Stockton)
Paisano Pass
(Alpine)

La Junta
(Presidio)

Chihuahua

GULF
OF
MEXICO

MEXICO

Charles D. Grear

unexplored region, there was a flurry of activity to investigate. Between 1839 and 1850 several expeditions were mounted to determine the course for roads, to evaluate the physical and biological aspects of the land, and to locate the resident and migratory Indians.

In 1839, Henry Connelly, a private entrepreneur, sought a route to Chihuahua that was shorter than the Missouri-Chihuahua trail. He set out across western Texas with eighty wagonloads of trade goods but the trip was a disaster. They passed through Gainesville, Nocona, Seymour, and Snyder on their way toward

El Paso.[8] The group got lost, encountered terrible weather, and in addition, the Mexican government changed while Connelly and his group were en route and imposed increased taxes on imports making the venture unprofitable.[9]

In 1848, commercial interests in San Antonio secured the services of a Texas Ranger, Colonel John C. (Jack) Hayes to lead an expedition seeking a suitable wagon route to El Paso, to join an existing road to Chihuahua, Mexico. And there were others. Although early travelers crossed the barren western lands long before Hays and Connelly, the private expeditions such as the one mounted by the citizens of San Antonio could not hope to provide the resources to make the sorts of evaluations needed by the federal government.

With increasing numbers of transients flooding through Texas en route to California, a second wave soon followed in their wake. These hardy souls wanted to establish homesteads in the western lands, a permanent relocation that would certainly be obnoxious to the indigenous peoples they would displace. These settlers demanded protection from their government in this tempestuous environment and soon their demands began to be heard. On March 20, 1848, the Texas state legislature passed a resolution requesting that the state's congressional delegation attempt to secure federal assistance, urging that Texas senators and representatives in Congress to use their influence for the passage of an act to establish "a chain of military posts in advance of the settlements, beyond Red River and Rio Grande. And that said posts shall be removed from time to time as the settlements advance."[10] The act also specified that US Indian agents and military commanders be required to confer with the governor of Texas so they could pursue appropriate policies jointly. Most Texans wanted the Indians to be dealt with severely, pushed outside the borders of the state, not only from the western frontier, and barring that, killed.

The federal government was not inclined to take such drastic measures. The nation already had an existing Indian policy, although support for it was divided. Some in Washington wanted to turn the Indians over to the army to manage, others, fearing that action would be tantamount to extermination, favored gradual assimilation through treaties and protected home ranges. In any respect, the federal government felt that Texas should be treated as any other state in terms of Indian policy.[11] Texans, however, felt differently. Unlike other states, Texas joined the union retaining all of its public lands. Texas law did not recognize Indian ownership of a single acre. The Texas legislature made requests to the federal government for more assistance not only in controlling the Indians but also the

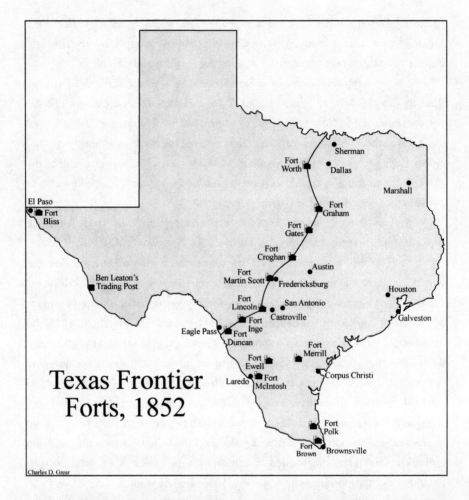

Texas Frontier
Forts, 1852

Charles D. Grear

various renegade bands who took advantage of the border instability and raided both sides of the Rio Grande.

The Secretary of War, William Learned Marcy, responded to the pressure from the Texas legislators. In December of 1848, Brevet Major General William J. Worth was sent to Texas to initiate a response. His plan was to station troops on the Rio Grande south of San Antonio and establish a cordon of seven military posts beginning at present Fort Worth in north Texas and extending across the state to the Mexican border at the Rio Grande. On December 5, 1848, the first post called Camp Houston (the name was later changed to Fort Martin Scott), was established two miles outside of Fredericksburg. Unfortunately, Worth did not live long enough to see his final plan realized because he died from cholera on May 7, 1849. [12]

Fort Inge was established on the Leona River in Uvalde County on March 13, 1849. These camps were followed by Croghan in Burnet, Lincoln near D'Hanis, Fort Graham near Hillsboro, and Fort Worth. The last camp in this first line of forts established in 1849 was Fort Gates, established on October 26 in present-day Coryell County. In addition, a series of posts were established on the Texas-Mexican border and included Fort Brown in present-day Brownsville, Ringgold Barracks near Rio Grande City, Fort McIntosh near Laredo, Duncan at Eagle Pass, and Fort Quitman fourteen miles south of present-day Sierra Blanco. These Rio Grande River forts terminated with a major facility at Fort Bliss in present-day El Paso.[13]

These outposts formed intersecting lines.[14] One, from Fort Worth to Fort Duncan on the Rio Grande, was to contain the settlers encroaching westward and prevent incursions from the Comanche and Kiowa Indians, whose territory was being invaded. Keeping these parties apart by a buffer zone of soldiers would keep the peace and discourage settlers from moving into the unprotected territories, both equally important issues from political and strategic standpoints. The river line of forts not only protected the US and Mexican frontier from invasions and raids by each nation's military, but also served as a trip wire defense and military cordon preventing Indians from raiding south of the Rio Grande, a duty assigned by Article 11 of the Treaty of Guadalupe Hidalgo.

This first line of forts was not adequate for long. The Indians, especially the Comanches and their allies, the Kiowas, did not abandon their hunting grounds easily.[15] The federal government underestimated the tenacity and aggressiveness of the Texas Indian population. Events would prove Indian determination: 38 percent of all Indian battles fought by federal forces before 1861 took place in Texas. Commanders in Washington soon learned that the troubles on the southern plains would not easily subside.[16]

Settlers also continued to push west, aggravating the situation. Indian unrest continued and even increased. General Worth began planning the next step needed to meet the needs of the settlers by initiating a series of expeditions surveying the frontier region of central west Texas, in anticipation of creating a second line of posts.

3

A Second Line of Forts

In 1849, Brevet Major General William J. Worth ordered Major Robert S. Neighbors to organize an expedition to evaluate the lands between the Pecos River and El Paso with the objective of determining suitability for troop movements. He was joined by Doctor John S. Ford of Austin.

In the same month, Lieutenants William H. C. Whiting and William F. Smith also successfully surveyed a route from San Antonio to El Paso. Whiting was only twenty-four years old at the time and in command of fifteen men. They left Fredericksburg in February traveling southwest, crossing the Pecos River, and arriving in El Paso after a narrow escape from Apache Indians. They returned by a route crossing the Devil's River, Las Moras Creek, the Nueces River, and the Rio Seco. The two engineers determined such a route would be suitable for wagons carrying cargo to El Paso from the Gulf of Mexico through San Antonio.

Three months after Whiting and Smith departed on their exploration Brevet Major Jefferson Van Horn departed San Antonio with six companies of the Third Infantry to further evaluate the "Lower" road Whiting used on his return from El Paso. It was constructed in the summer of 1849 and used for many years.

There were other expeditions that year because of the need for a road connecting the depot at Fort Smith, Arkansas, with El Paso. A second journey by Whiting came near the future locations of a second tier of posts, but it was left to the command in Fort Smith, Arkansas, to determine the route of a future road from Fort Smith to El Paso. An expedition from Fort Smith would play an important role in the selection of the future site of Fort Phantom Hill. The man they selected to lead the military escort was Captain Randolph B. Marcy.

The US military presence in Arkansas and Texas long pre-dated the Civil War. Fort Smith, Arkansas, was established initially in 1817 to maintain a watch on Indian Territory. It was abandoned in 1824. The post was reestablished in 1836 when Congress, in response to the changing defense situation, made appropriations that would keep the base functioning as a supply depot of other posts in the southwest and for military units that were traveling through the area.[1] Additionally, at the beginning of the Mexican War, the post equipped US military units heading to battle across the Rio Grande. When the war in Mexico ended, the security offered by the post attracted hundreds of men and women who gathered there before heading to the gold fields of California.

Fort Smith also served as the administrative office for Indian affairs in Texas and other western areas and as a base for the various reconnaissance expeditions into those areas. The fort was the supply depot for new military posts that would later be built in Oklahoma and Texas.[2] By 1849, Fort Smith became the headquarters of the Seventh Military Department and was commanded by Brevet Brigadier General Matthew Arbuckle.

Another major installation was the headquarters of the Eighth Military Department in San Antonio, commanded in 1849 by General George M. Brooke. Both divisions were to have new commanders at nearly the same time. In San Antonio, when General Brooke died in 1851, Brigadier General William S. Harney became the temporary commander pending the arrival of Major General Persifor F. Smith; in Fort Smith, General Arbuckle was succeeded by General William Goldsmith Belknap.[3]

In addition to Fort Smith and San Antonio, two other locations would play an early role in the future founding of the Camp on the Brazos: Fort Washita and Fort Towson in Indian Territory. Fort Washita, located near present Durant, Oklahoma, was established by General Zachary Taylor. He rode into Indian Territory some eighty miles beyond the existing military location at Fort Townsend to pinpoint the location for a new fort for the protection of the Choctaws and Chickasaws against marauding plains Indians. The new fort was constructed by Company D of the Fifth Infantry on the location selected by Marcy, and by 1842 it was occupied by forces of Companies A and F of the Second Dragoons.

Fort Smith photo ca. 1850. Courtesy of the National Park Service online archives; www.nps.gov/fosm/.../postcards-of-second-fort-smith.htm.

Lieutenant Clinton W. Lear and Captain Marcy were among the officers stationed at Fort Washita. The availability of a neat row of officers' quarters at the facility meant that the men's wives could accompany them and soon there was a lively social life among the women. Lear and Marcy, however, were soon to be transferred to the frontier in Texas. Fort Washita became a major location from which numerous excursions were made.

In 1849, the government dispatched Captain Marcy to find another route through Texas. Marcy was an unusual man. A gifted explorer, he traversed the western lands repeatedly, gathering scientific information, surveying, and reporting on the indigenous Indians he encountered. Born in Greenwich, Massachusetts, in 1812, he entered West Point on July 1, 1828, and graduated a Brevet Second Lieutenant on July 1, 1832. Marcy first saw frontier duty when he was sent to Fort Towson, Indian Territory, in 1848 and remained in the west in a variety of locations until he was assigned to Florida during the Seminole wars. He was the author of three books, including *The Prairie Traveler*, a guide to expedition preparation. He retired after forty years of service as a brigadier general.

Even though there was a national incentive to establish roads and rail service to the west coast, Marcy's expedition came about in part through the activity of the local newspaper in Fort Smith. Hoping to develop the importance of the community, the editor suggested establishing a road that would begin in Fort

Lieutenant Frederick Dent. Courtesy of the Prints and Photographs Division, Library of Congress; Photograph No. LC-USZ62LC-DIG-cwpbh-00678, Brady-Handy Photograph Collection.

Randolph Marcy. Prints and Photographs Division, Library of Congress. Brady-Handy Photograph Collection. http://hdl.loc.gov/loc.pnp/cwpbh.03149. LC-BH831-920[P&P].

Smith and continue to California, thereby creating increased activity for the growing community. The idea caught fire. The proposal was approved by the Secretary of War, George Walker Crawford, and the responsibility to organize the force was given to Colonel Matthew Arbuckle at Fort Smith. Arbuckle sent Lieutenant Frederick T. Dent of the Fifth Infantry, who would later become commander of Company G at Fort Phantom Hill, to reconnoiter a route for a future road to Santa Fe as they accompanied the travelers westward.

Captain Marcy was selected to lead the expedition with troops from the Fifth Infantry. He received his orders on April 2, 1849 and immediately prepared to leave for Santa Fe. As word spread, Fort Smith swelled with gold seekers and other travelers awaiting the military escort. Marcy left with a detachment from the Fifth Infantry along with the emigrants on April 4, 1849.[4]

The expedition traveled a wide loop seeking a practical route between Fort Smith and Santa Fe and included passage through present-day Oklahoma and Texas. This path was somewhat longer but enjoyed better weather than a

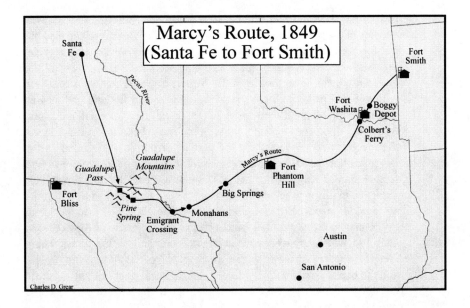

more northern route and the Indian population was more remote and less threatening. It was not the most popular route west, but it did add much to the overall understanding of the geography of northwest Texas and suggested possible uses for this country in the decades ahead. The expedition crossed the Canadian River and paralleled it, leading toward Santa Fe. In addition to determining the feasibility of the route, Marcy was to "conciliate" the Indians he encountered and make an investigation of the countryside. He was instructed to keep a detailed journal of each day's journey and give protection to the immigrants he encountered on the trip.

On his return trip from Santa Fe, Marcy decided to take a more southern route, steering clear of the northern area more heavily populated by the Indians and their potential threat. He crossed the Delaware Mountains at Guadalupe Pass, skirting the base of El Capitan, and camped for the night at Pine Springs. The route then continued east. When the expedition arrived at the Pecos River, on the advice of his Comanche guide, Manuel, they followed the western bank of the Pecos River for nearly fifty miles before crossing at what became known in later years as the Emigrant Crossing.

Marcy recorded the crossing and the ingenuity required to improvise wagons as makeshift ferries.

> September 21st—I was obliged to resort to one of those expedients which necessity often forces travelers in this wild country to put in practice; and that was, to invent and construct a substitute for a ferry-

boat to transport our men and baggage across the river [the Pecos]. This I did by taking one of our wagon beds and placing six empty barrels in it, lashing them down firmly with ropes, and by tying one on each outside, opposite the centre. I then attached a long stout rope to each end of the bed, and placed it bottom up in the water; a man then swam the river with the end of a small cord in his mouth, and to the end of this was tied one of the tops of the wagon, which he pulled across and made fast to a stake upon the opposite bank. Some men then took passage upon the inverted wagon boats, and the current carried it to the other shore, the rope attached to the stake preventing it from going down the stream further than its length. The boat was then drawn back by men for another load, and in this manner we crossed our men and baggage in a short time. We could transport two thousand pounds of freight at one load, perfectly dry. Our wagons were then lashed fast to the axles, with ropes tied to each end, when they were pushed into the river and hauled across. There were fifteen feet of water where we crossed. As the current ran rapidly and the banks were muddy and steep, I was fearful that our mules would not make the passage. I therefore tied a rope to the neck of each one and pulled them across.[5]

After crossing the Pecos, the expedition then struggled through the sand hills near Monahans and, with Manuel's expertise, found water and firm ground. Somewhere at this point in their travels, Manuel returned to New Mexico and Black Beaver, the well-known Delaware Indian, translator and chief, guided the men to Big Spring and on to the conclusion of the trip.

The expedition then passed the Double Mountain Fork of the Brazos River in present-day Stonewall County, Texas and continued on to the junction of the Clear Fork and the main channel of the Brazos River. Largely because of the skill of Black Beaver, they were able to find adequate water and forage for the animals but the trip was not uneventful. Although the expedition was camped in the vicinity of present-day Colorado City, on October 7, 1849, Lieutenant Montgomery P. Harrison hiked down to examine a ravine after dinner and did not return. The next day, a search party found his scalped and mangled body thrown down into the rocks, murdered by Kiowa Indians. It was a tragic reminder that the lands they traversed were still claimed by the nomadic Indian buffalo hunters.

On October 14, the expedition was hit by a sudden drop in temperature, a "blue norther" that continued with a heavy rain, drenching the men and causing the creeks to overflow their banks. Marcy's report states that thirty-three mules froze to death. The delays caused the rations to run short and Marcy had to reduce the amount of flour distributed by one-fourth. By the time the men reached the Clear Fork, the Indians had received advance notice by a series of smoke signals. The guide, Black Beaver, went ahead and established contact with an encampment of Senaco's Comanches who were friendly. Encounters with several of the different groups of Indians caused Marcy to note in his report on his return to Fort Smith that the area of the Clear Fork seemed to be an appropriate location for a new military post. He further noted that the southern route was the best appropriate location for the road to the west. Additionally, the swollen streams they crossed and the abundance of game and forage indicated to Marcy that the land was well watered and would sustain a military outpost. How could Marcy have known that the year 1849 was exceptional in terms of rainfall and the scarcity of potable water would be one of the greatest disadvantages of the site that was finally selected?[6]

After Marcy established his trail between Fort Smith and Santa Fe, the Eighth Military Department commander, Brevet Major General Brooke, ordered Whiting to make another investigation closer to the existing forts of the first line and to report on their status, needs, and the possible location of roads to connect the defenses.

Whiting received his orders on October 1, 1849, and traveled north from Fort Duncan on the Rio Grande to the Red River near Denison. He passed Fort Martin Scott, Forts Croghan, Gates, Graham, and Worth. From there, at Coffee's Bend, they traveled west across the southern plains, crossed the Pecos at the Horsehead Crossing, and continued to El Paso.

In his report of January 1, 1850, to General Brooke, Whiting suggested additional equipment ensuring the troops would be in an increased state of readiness, noting that the posts were undermanned for the mission, but the land was desirable for settlement. He described the land he passed through and wrote "It was attractive to Indians because of abundant game and shelter from northers." Whiting recommended the addition of two thousand mounted troops for border protection, noting that foot soldiers did not impress the mounted Indians. Whiting also believed there would be little settlement beyond the "arable lands and the sterile plains of the northwest."[7]

Whiting specifically suggested two additional forts be constructed, one on the Red River and another on the Brazos. In March of the same year, he supplemented the previous report with warnings of continued border trouble, suggesting that troops stationed at the forts with only foot soldiers had a lack of rapid mobility and could never cope with the mounted and versatile Indian foes. He recommended the substitution of light cavalry for the infantry, to be located

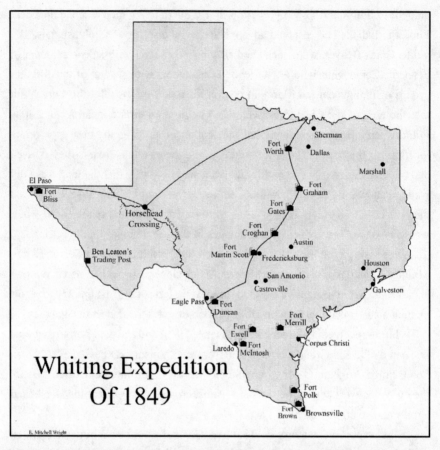

Whiting Expedition
Of 1849

E. Mitchell Wright

where the Indians lived, and the relentless pursuit and destruction of the Indians, their families, and camps. Although his suggestions went unheeded at the time, they had been heard.

While these surveys were taking place, the citizens continued to be harassed. By June of 1850, Captain Marcy, familiar with the area from his previous expeditions, was directed to select the site for a new installation near the Canadian River to be named Camp Arbuckle to protect this area, but Camp Arbuckle was not destined for a long occupation by federal forces, and because the location was deemed to be unhealthy, the permanent fort was constructed several miles away. The raids continued.

In September 1850, the Comanche Indians initiated attacks along the center of the frontier.[8] When General Brooke focused his defense on the center of the line, the Indians moved to the southern end. At the same time, negotiations began with the Indians to end the hostilities. Both groups met near Fredericksburg and signed

peace treaties. A boundary was established following the east side of
the Colorado River near the existing posts. It did not last long. The
War Department finally came to
the conclusion in early 1851 that
more force was necessary to deal
with the Indian situation.

On June 5, 1851, the Assistant
Adjutant General, Colonel Samuel Cooper, visited the Indian villages near the Clear Fork to evaluate their peaceful intent and their
conditions. Major Henry Hopkins
Sibley of the Second Dragoons
from Fort Graham commanded
his escort.

William H. C. Whiting. Courtesy of the Prints and
Photographs Division, Library of Congress; Photo No.
LC-B813- 1416 A; http://hdl.loc.gov/loc.pnp/cwpb.04918.

After marching four days to
the northwest by way of Barnard's Trading Post, continuing
past Comanche and Bald Head
peaks and Fish Eating Creek, the
expedition arrived at the Kichai
Indian village on the left bank of
the Brazos. The area was a rich
river valley with a Caddo village
situated across the river about fifteen miles below the junction of
the Clear Fork.

Cooper and Sibley crossed
to the Caddo Village on the west
bank and returned by way of
Comanche Peak and Barnard's
Trading Post. The circuit covered some 250 miles of highly
variable landscape. There were

William F. Smith. Courtesy of the Prints and Photographs
Division, Library of Congress; LC-B813- 2160 A [P&P]
LOT 4192; http://hdl.loc.gov/loc.pnp/cwpb.06368.

Kichai
Village

Caddo
Village

Clear Fork of the Brazos

Fort
Phantom
Hill

Abilene

Comanche
Peak

Barnard's
Trading
Post

Brazos River

Fort
Graham

Waco

**Colonel Samuel Cooper and
Major Henry Hopkins Sibley's
Expedition, 1851**

Charles D. Grear

high plains and tablelands cut by deep gorges that required careful maneuvering to cross.

Typically, each of the tribes they visited had its own chief and each was friendly and hospitable to the group. The tribes were agriculturalists and grew large quantities of corn and vegetables, but their primary support came from buffalo, which had been scarce. The people were starving, which may have accounted for their friendliness. They wanted help from the federal government.

In his report to his superiors, Cooper recommended that a military post be established on the Clear Fork near the Caddo village not only to protect the white settlers in the area but also the resident Indians.[9]

The Comanches had become a particular problem for several reasons. In 1849, a cholera epidemic wiped out more than three hundred members of the northern and southern branches of the Comanche, killing among others, the two principal chiefs, Old Owl and Santa Ana, both of whom were inclined to peaceful relations with "The Great White Father." Neither man was officially in charge of the various bands, but the respect in which they were held enabled the two chiefs to restrain the bands from hostilities. One of the exceptions to those with peaceful inclinations was the Southern Comanche chief Buffalo Hump. He definitely created problems by encouraging his people to oppose the European settlers whom he accused of driving away the buffalo and encroaching on his historic territory.[10]

With Indian problems continuing, citizens resorted to personal efforts with the administration. Jane Cazneau, a creative adventuress who lived in Eagle Pass, went to Washington to lobby for more frontier protection. It was reported that when she met with President Millard Fillmore, she chastised him about the "terrible state of the frontier."[11]

Cazneau felt it shameful that only infantry were present to defend the people and suggested that the government employ the Seminole Indian Chief Wild Cat to institute a cooperative program of defense using members of his tribe who had taken refuge in Mexico. She thought the government might "assign his band a home and rations," enabling him to create "a humane, politic, and

Colonel Samuel Cooper. Courtesy of National Portrait Gallery, Smithsonian Institution. NPG.98.92.

economical border militia of the friendly tribes." She said, "We owe something very different to the Indians than the mockery of fifths of rum and treaties of specious promises."[12]

The sense of frustration with the slow pace of governmental action galled the settlers who were facing the brunt of Indian attacks. They could only persevere and rely on their own resources and occasional help from the scattered Texas state militias. However, help was coming. The bureaucracy was shifting gears.

In 1851, both General Harney and General Brooke before him, in San Antonio, along with General Arbuckle in Fort Smith, were asked by the citizens to respond to the need for additional frontier protection for transients and settlers.

Although he was only an interim commander, Harney took firm control of department affairs, sending Lieutenant W. J. Hardee on an expedition against the Indians; rearranging the locations of the troops to more adequately defend the frontier; and establishing Fort Mason, near present Mason, Texas, the location of which was selected with the assistance of Richard Austin Howard, a San Antonio surveyor who also owned or had an interest in the future sites of Forts Chadbourne and Clark.[13]

In Fort Smith, Brevet Brigadier General Arbuckle was succeeded by General Belknap. [14] On June 12, 1851, Belknap was given orders from Assistant Quartermaster General Henry Stanton in St. Louis to determine locations and establish posts to form a second line of defense following an order from the War Department. These orders likely reflected conversations the previous April between Stanton and Arbuckle. Rationally, the logistics for developing any new line of fortifications would issue from that command.

Belknap, although a capable officer, was evidently not well regarded by his subordinates. On September 23, 1850, a letter to Clinton Lear from his friend, Lieutenant Fred Meyers, one of the junior officers at Camp Arbuckle, shed some light on the opinion of at least one person regarding his superior General Belknap. "A report at [Fort] Washita is that Genl Belknap is in arrest, disobedience of orders."[15] Previously in a letter to his wife, Lear expressed his opinion of Belknap when he stated, "Mr. Myers left this morning for Gibson to assume the duties of Regtl. Quarter Master. I do not envy him. It is certain I would not get along with old Belknap."[16]

Fort Washita was the focal point for the organization of the expedition to establish the two new posts and seven companies of the Fifth Infantry assembled there. Captain Marcy was included because of his experience in 1849 mapping the same territory. In addition, the guide for the mission was Black Beaver, the well-known Delaware Indian who guided Marcy's previous journey. Marcy's friends, Lear and Second Lieutenant Ben Wingate, were also included in the group.

Strangely, the orders given Arbuckle and Belknap overlapped those given to the commander of the new Eighth Military Department, General Persifor F. Smith. On April 30, 1851, the Secretary of War C. M. Conrad wrote General Smith, who was scheduled to succeed General Brooke as the commander of the newly organized Texas (Eighth Military) Department, making him responsible for supervising the construction of the first of the forts to be built establishing the second line of defense and to determine how many posts would be constructed and where they would be located.

General Arbuckle, however, sent conflicting instructions to Brevet Lieutenant Colonel William Wallace Smith Bliss in New Orleans that verified the posts were to be established by the Fifth Infantry from Fort Smith.[17] Conflict was certain to occur as each of the generals would have his own opinion regarding the locations of the proposed forts.

On June 24, 1851, General Belknap, accompanied by Marcy and Company C of the Fifth Infantry began their expedition to scout the territory and determine the location of the future posts. They reached the Salt Fork of the Brazos where Belknap determined it would be the site of the first post. Later it moved two miles down stream for better water. (later renamed Fort Belknap). Advised of the death of General Arbuckle, Belknap returned to Fort Smith to assume command of the Seventh Military Department. He instructed Marcy to continue his explorations as far as Pecan Bayou where he envisioned the site for the second post. Marcy departed the Brazos on July 1 and continued as far south as Pecan Bayou and determined the second post should be situated there. In Marcy's response of November 25, 1851, to the request of the Adjutant General's Office, in Washington, he described his observations and the proposed site:

> At the base of the mountains I struck an old Indian trail which led me by a gentle ascent along the valley of the small creek to the summit of the pass, and from thence descending by an easy and regular grade for ten miles it brought me into the valley of "Pecan Bayou." This stream rises about thirty miles above where I struck it, and as I have before remarked runs a southeast course into the Colorado. As General Belknap designed (if practicable) to establish the second post in this line upon this stream, I made a very minute and careful examination of the country in the vicinity for about forty miles below the forks, and found it as I have described on pages (11) and (12) of this report. The point when I first arrived at the creek is the highest position that I could discover, where a good site for a military post, with all the materials for building, and other requisites for a garrison can be had, as above tis point the timber is scarce and in a few miles almost entirely disappears.[18]

Belknap began plans to construct the first fort in the second line where he and Marcy selected the location and ordered Major J. J. Abercrombie to proceed with a detachment to begin the work on both forts. The second of these was to be the future Fort Phantom Hill.

4

Establishing a Post on the Brazos River

Major J. J. Abercrombie was certainly capable of dealing with the trackless and dry West Texas prairie. A West Point graduate of English lineage, he was born in Tennessee. A veteran officer, he served in both the Seminole war in Florida and with Zachary Taylor in Mexico, winning his first commendation for bravery during the campaign against the Seminoles. He received a brevet commission to lieutenant colonel for bravery and meritorious service during the Monterrey campaign. At the end of the Mexican War, he was assigned to serve on the frontier in Texas, Arkansas, and the Indian Territory.

Accompanying Major Abercrombie was a civilian employee, W. Jeff Maltby. Born in Sangamon County, Illinois, in 1829, he came to the southwest to seek his fortune. Settlement of the Texas frontier in the mid-1800s was not for the timid or the inept, but Maltby was neither. In his memoir, he modestly describes himself as being "six-foot-high, with breast and shoulders of a lion" and weighing two hundred pounds. His size and self-confidence would serve him well as he sought adventure on the western frontier. When the Belknap expedition from Fort Smith was launched to establish several of the forts, Maltby was placed in charge of the livestock that would accompany the troops.[1] The expedition to establish the line of forts would be hard on the mules and oxen; they would be required to graze

35

Major J. J. Abercrombie. Courtesy of the Prints and Photographs Division, Library of Congress; Photo No. LCB813B; cwpbo5128.

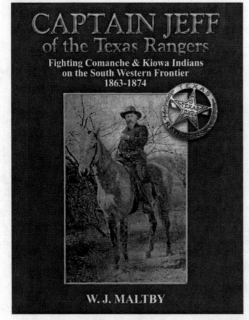

W. J. Maltby. *Captain Jeff or Frontier Life in Texas with the Texas Rangers.*

for food at camps along the way where grass and water were uncertain.

Before reaching Texas to establish the first post, the expedition split. Several men and teams were diverted to Shreveport, along with Maltby, to acquire some additional supplies. Abercrombie and the remainder of the command continued on toward the Red River where they would join up again.

Upon their arrival in Shreveport, Maltby was promoted to engineer and put in charge of a six-pound brass cannon, along with a team of six fine gray mules. He was responsible for the cannon and its caisson for the rest of the trip.

After securing the cannon and supplies, the detachment followed the right bank of the Red River until meeting the route taken by the rest of the command, following that trail to the Preston settlement at Coffey's Bend.[2]

Major Abercrombie crossed the Red River at Preston where the combined command continued to a location General Belknap selected about ten miles below the Marcy Brazos River crossing where they established Camp Brazos on June 24, 1851.

In his report of July 7, to the Adjutant General of the Seventh

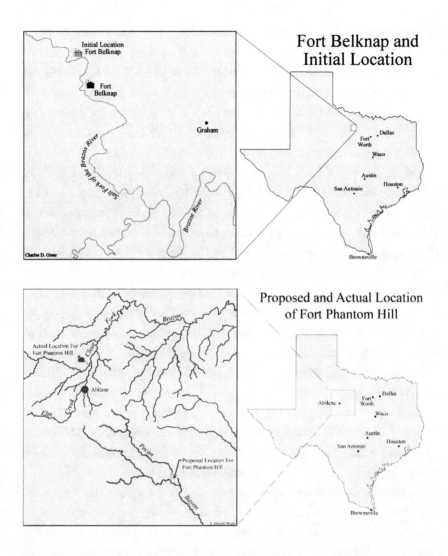

Military department, Belknap described the location of the site of the first post, calling it the farthest west a fort could be constructed because of the scarcity of wood for the construction. He reported, "This should judge to be about the one hundreth degree of West Longitude . . ."[3]

While Abercrombie was busy establishing the first fort in the second line according to his orders, Brevet Major General Persifor F. Smith prepared to assume his command in San Antonio. On September 16, 1851, General Smith took command of the Eighth Military Deparment and soon afterward left San Antonio on an exploratory trip to evaluate sites for the new forts his instructions ordered him to establish. The defense of the Northwest Texas frontier had been switched from Belknap to Smith, perhaps without Belknap's knowledge. The Secretary of War C. M. Conrad ordered Smith to establish the line of posts originally assigned to the Seventh Military Department. Before leaving San Antonio, he had examined the maps and planned the location of the posts without seeing the country. En route to meet Belknap, he made a cursory survey of the territory, which did not alter his preconceived plans.

Passing south of the site chosen by Belknap and Marcy for the second fort in the line, General Smith crossed the Concho River and the Red Fork of the Colorado. On November 3, Smith arrived on the Salt Fork of the Brazos where he met Belknap and Marcy, who had returned from Fort Smith, and Major Abercrombie, where they were camped and in the process of construction of the first post. Smith informed Belknap that he was now responsible for the site location of the proposed posts. The generals compared notes on their own ideas regarding the proposed locations. Belknap proposed his selection for the site for the second fort on Pecan Bayou that Marcy visited earlier in the year, where both agreed the location was excellent.

General Smith had other ideas. He envisioned the location of the first of the new forts, the Camp on the Brazos, some twenty miles from where Belknap had already located it. After arriving at the site, he decided to let it stay where it was. General Smith then decided one additional camp would suffice and that it should be located at a site on the Clear Fork, some seventy miles distant from Fort Belknap but not at the location selected previously by General Belknap and Marcy.

Evidently, though history does not record it, there must have been some powerful discussions between the two generals when, without visiting Belknap's previous choice, Smith moved the location of the second site from Pecan Bayou to a location he described as "on my route being at the junction of the two branches of the Clear Fork and near many villages of Indians laying a little east of the position. . . ." His actual route, following the old Marcy trail, was actually two miles south of the site he proposed.

As Smith's Eighth Military District had just been extended all the way north to the Red River, his decision prevailed. Smith disregarded suggestions that the water of the Clear Fork was actually not clear (at that location) and was generally unsuitable to drink. He stubbornly refused to change his decision, believing his primitive map showed adequate water and timber.[4] This conflict between the two sets of orders and the change of jurisdiction was to result in the unfortunate location of the second fort in the new line that contributed to its abandonment only two and a half years later.

After the conference, the two generals departed. Belknap headed to Fort Washita whereas Smith returned to San Antonio. General Belknap had been ill since arriving at the meeting, possibly affecting his reaction to the decision regarding the second camp. His condition was noted by General Smith in a letter to William Wallace Smith Bliss, the Assistant Adjutant General of the Western Division. Smith noted "[o]n arriving here I found Gen. Belknap very sick with a dysentery he has been afflicted with since he left Fort Smith. . . . Gen. Belknap, if able to travel, will go to some post where there are barracks. . . . his physicians think that the exposure any longer to cold nights & hot days will be fatal."[5] The meeting with General Smith could well have been so stressful that it tipped Belknap over the edge. In a letter to his wife Mary, Lieutenant William Clinton Lear reported: "The Gen'l is quite sick and I would not be surprised if he never returns to the Regt." [6] Belknap must have been even sicker than Lear and Smith suspected, for he died near Preston while en route to Fort Washita. Mary Rossell described the circumstances in a gossipy letter to her friend Mary Lear:

> On Monday morning Dr. Baily, Mr Myers and Mr Burns arrived in the rain. Mr. Burns going after his wife & Capt. Sibley's family, and with directions to bring me on with them if I choose to go as Gen Bel[k]nap was back a few miles very sick, would be here in an hour. Mr Nuba and several soldiers were with him. Dr. Baily said the only chance for his life was to get him here, have him quiet & well nursed and he was entirely out of his head. The day as I said before was horrible, and we all felt very gloomy to know that the poor sick old man was out in the storm. We all became very anxious, as four o'clock came and he did not appear, at last—Doctor Madison (he was to be placed there) started out in his wagon after him, went one mile, met the ambulance and horrible to relate Gen. Belknap was a corpse. He had died about twelve o'clock without a struggle, but perfectly unconscious of his situation. The tongue of the wagon broke and his attendant got out to assist, and was only out ten minutes—when he stepped into the wagon Gen. Belnap [sic] was dead. His corpse was brought in, laid in the house Mrs. Abercorombie [sic] had when here, and buried on Monday at 4 o'clock in the enclosure by the garden and at the side of your own dear little boy. . . . Dr. Baily says he has had great trouble of mind, many things worried him & the change made by Gen. Smith annoyed him much. . . .[7]

After General Smith prevailed in the decision regarding the location of the second fort, orders were given to Lieutenant Colonel Abercrombie to lead the construction team to erect the fort on the upper Brazos River. In the general order issued on November 3, General Smith cited the location as "Phantom Hill" and later, in a letter, Major Abercrombie referred to the site as "the Phantom Bluff."[8] This indicated the place name was known before the actual construction of the post.

On November 6, 1851, Major Abercrombie left Camp Belknap with 231 men in five companies of the Fifth Infantry. They were accompanied by fifty horses, plus mules and oxen to build the second fort in the new line of defense. For the second stage of the expedition, Abercrombie secured the services of Black Beaver, Chief of the Delaware Indians, as a guide. Black Beaver, a guide for the previous Marcy Expedition, was widely regarded as dependable and familiar with the territory.

This land beyond the Cross Timbers, as the wooded region west and north of present Dallas was called, separated much of the settled part of Texas from the rolling plains and Chihuahuan Desert of the western areas. If a traveler of today were transported back in time, he or she would think it was a different country. Where today there are farms and fences, mesquite thickets and broad highways, in 1851 there was endless grass to the horizon, transitioning to desert shrub beyond present Midland. The only trees bordered the intermittent creeks that drained the area. Travelers unfamiliar with the scarce landmarks were forced to rely on a compass to keep their bearings and even then it was easy to lose their way.

Because it is difficult to visualize the character of the countryside 150 years after the journey, it is important to develop an understanding of the circumstances the expedition encountered in establishing the fort. Michael Baldridge, a member of a French expedition en route to the gold fields of California crossed western Texas and described the countryside as follows:

> After we had left the settlements, we had then to pass through six hundred miles of uninhabited country, over the wilds and table-lands of western Texas, where Indian John was monarch of all he surveyed, and his right there were none to dispute. Here we left the rain and mosquitos behind us, and were never troubled with them more. And here we found a climate where beef could be cured and dried as hard as horn, in the hot sun and open air, and not spoil. A little farther on we found a scenery, soil and climate that was all that could have been desired in the Garden of Eden. If it had been located there, however, appearances indicated that it had been sadly neglected, and that the serpent family had held possession there since our first parents left it. It was indeed a beautiful

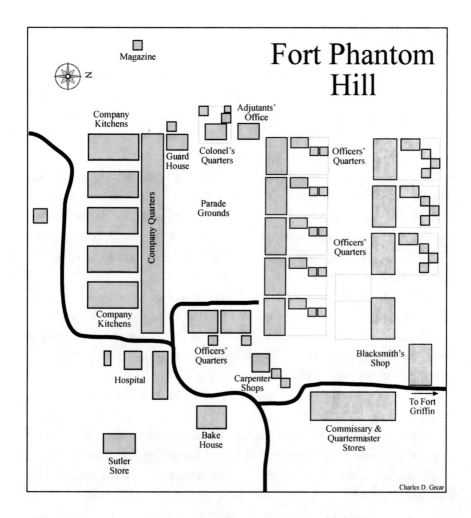

Fort Phantom Hill

Magazine

Company Kitchens

Adjutants' Office

Guard House

Colonel's Quarters

Officers' Quarters

Company Quarters

Parade Grounds

Officers' Quarters

Company Kitchens

Officers' Quarters

Blacksmith's Shop

Hospital

Carpenter Shops

To Fort Griffin

Bake House

Commissary & Quartermaster Stores

Sutler Store

Charles D. Grear

country, but the chief population was rattlesnakes. Several of our people were bitten by them and we were compelled to coil a hair rope around the tent at night in case we objected to having them for bedfellows I will not attempt to estimate the number per acre, as a very near approximate to the truth would surely be regarded as a snake story.[9]

With the camp equipment transported by wagons drawn by the oxen and mule teams, the men set out on Captain Marcy's existing trail toward Santa Fe that followed the north side of the Clear Fork of the Brazos River.

The third night after leaving Fort Belknap, the party found an ideal camping spot located somewhere southwest of the present-day town of Graham, Texas, described by Maltby in his journal as "a beautiful basin surrounded by mountains." Because they had to depend on the prairie grass for forage, the mules and oxen were turned loose early in the morning and allowed to graze. A guard was posted to watch the stock during the night, and Maltby took the last watch with two others. About daylight, orders were given to hitch up the wagons, but Black Beaver was worried about the weather. He approached Abercrombie to tell him they should stay because a major storm was approaching.

The major, secure in his belief that his fine hack and pair of strong black horses would carry him forward without a problem, told the experienced guide that he would go ahead and the rest of the party could follow his tracks when he turned off the old Marcy trail. By "good daylight" he was gone with Black Beaver and the accompanying soldiers, instructing the wagon masters and Maltby to follow at a certain time.

Major Abercrombie must have believed that the tracks could be easily followed. He was wrong. When the rest of the party decamped with the wagons and the cannon, a storm hit with incredible force. The quartermaster, who was in charge of leading the group, came to the place he thought he had been directed to turn off from the Marcy trail and travel westward.

Maltby, with the caisson, followed close behind the quartermaster and the major's baggage took up the rear. They soon came to a canyon they could not cross and realized they had turned from the Marcy trail too soon. There was but one solution: retrace their tracks to the Marcy Trail, placing them squarely into the onslaught of the sleet, hail, and freezing rain of the storm. Maltby described the hail as coming with as much force as having been shot from a cannon.

Somehow with a superhuman effort, the party led by the quartermaster made it back to the old Marcy Trail they left some time before. Maltby and his drovers ran beside their teams and urged them onward, but soon any forward progress was impossible and the men were in serious danger of freezing. Maltby describes the ordeal as follows:

> When we had got back to where we had left the trail the quartermaster said, "Boys, for God sake, try to make a fire, for I believe we shall all freeze to death." And then the language he used about his commanding officer for not leaving a guide to direct him, would not do to put in print. There was an ax in the Major's baggage wagon and some dry material. John White, the driver, got them out, and as there was plenty of dry mesquite trees at the spot, I took the ax and went to splitting up wood

with a will, urged on by the necessity. The two other drivers kindled a fire and in a short time we had a life-giving blaze. The drivers brought up their wagons, jumped off their saddle mules and hovered over the fire.[10]

The quartermaster had continued on, ahead of the rest of the group, searching for the trail left by Major Abercrombie. Maltby heard a shout in the distance and threw down his ax, raced to his team, grabbed the reins and, running beside the freezing mules, whipped them forward. Finally he came upon the quartermaster and followed him into the major's camp.

The major had named the place "Camp Necessity" because his fine horses refused to go any farther and he had to stop. When he was asked why he had chosen such an exposed and inappropriate location, Major Thomas replied, "It was a military necessity." Being forced to stop was fortunate in one respect because if the major's group had been able to travel farther, the quartermaster and the rest of the command might have perished trying to find them.

Fortunately, the soldiers had constructed good fires. When Maltby and the quartermaster reached the camp, the quartermaster was so frozen he could not dismount and had to be lifted from his horse and carried to the fire. The doctor provided him with a shot of brandy, rubbed his body, and saved his life.

Within a couple of hours, twenty or thirty wagons arrived, but the wagon master still had not come. It was mass confusion. Without him to give instructions to the drivers, they turned their mules loose and the animals drifted away from camp in the storm. Some of the teamsters brought in their teams and left the wagons behind. Some had blankets in their wagons and simply released their animals, then crawled into the wagons and pulled the covers over their heads. The next day, Maltby recruited Bill Stevens, a young teamster, to go with him in search of the wandering mules. The two found the animals but were unable to drive them back alone so they began walking back to camp.

Black Beaver appeared and they asked where he was going. "Back to camp," he replied. "Oh no," they said, pointing in another direction. "Camp is this way." He replied: "You go your way, I go mine," while riding away. Maltby and Stevens wisely decided to follow, soon arriving in camp. It they had taken their own heading, they would surely have been lost and frozen to death that same night. [11]

When Maltby and Stevens arrived in camp, three or four more teamsters arrived riding their saddle mules, having left their wagons and turning the rest of the saddle mules loose. They were concerned that James Morehead, their companion, had not arrived, and feared he would freeze to death.

Billy Benton, a nephew of Senator Thomas Hart Benton of Missouri, requested a horse of William Locklin, the wagon master, volunteering to ride to Morehead's assistance and bring him back to camp. All advised the lad not to go because the conditions were dangerous.

Benton said, "Morehead shall not freeze to death if I can save him." He mounted his horse and rode five miles into the storm where he found Morehead sitting down, so cold he was speechless. Benton tried to lift him onto the horse but was unable to do so. He remounted and returned to camp to get assistance. Maltby, William Kemper, and William Lacy responded. They caught four mules, hitched them to an unloaded wagon, put in a kettle of hot coals from the fires and secured a bottle of brandy from the doctor. Kemper rode the saddle mule, Lacy climbed into the wagon and positioned himself by the kettle of hot coals. Maltby led the head mule by the bridle, and they started back to rescue Morehead.

They found him lying on his back on the ground. They quickly hoisted him into the wagon near the hot coals and poured brandy down his throat. Unfortunately their efforts were in vain, and Morehead died from exposure, after which Maltby grasped the lead mule's bridle again and walked the wagon back to camp. They arrived about midnight. Maltby reported that a kindly hand presented him with a steaming cup of coffee, the only drink he had since the morning before. He traveled on foot for more than forty miles in the biting storm in the past two days without food.

The next day was clear and Maltby was ready to eat. "We rustled up some fat pickled pork, soldier hard tack and coffee, of which I ate about one pound of raw, fat pork, five or six hard tacks and drank a quart of strong coffee, and then felt equal to any" he wrote in his book.

After breakfast the party set out to recover the wandering animals. They traveled on horseback and by foot and by ten o'clock most of the mules were caught, although many had died in the storm.

After hooking up teams they went back to bring in the wagons and the men who were left behind in the storm. It was not until night that all were back in Camp Necessity, where they got another square meal and buried Morehead, who as Maltby mused in his journal, "like many thousands, had lost his life in trying to carry out an unnecessary military order."[12]

The following morning the group left Camp Necessity and about noon, thanks to the guideship of Black Beaver, they reached a good natural ford across the

Clear Fork of the Brazos. The major drove over and Maltby followed with the cannon. When they reached the top of a rise, a beautiful hill covered with trees was sighted and the group moved in that direction.

"The major drover and I followed him with my cannon," Maltby wrote. "When he reached the rise of the south bank about one mile southwest, a beautiful hill covered with beautiful trees was plain in sight. We moved forward to it, and as we approached it the hill and trees became less and less. When the Major got near it, he halted, called his officers, got out of this hack, and they, with Black Beaver, walked all over the little hill and grove, and when he returned he said, 'Here we locate Fort Phantom Hill, for this is one spot where distance lends enchantment to the view'Hence the name, Phantom Hill."[13]

On Friday, November 14, 1851, after reaching the location of Phantom Hill with companies C and G, Abercrombie proceeded with the construction of the camp. Companies B, E, and K were left behind to bury Morehead and the animals killed in the storm. They arrived at the site two days later.[14] The site was located on a gently rolling hill with scattered mesquites and a small five-acre grove of blackjack oak that struggled in the thin, gravelly soil.[15]

Upon their arrival, the men first began to search for a source of water and then for building materials. The immediate concern was water. The Clear Fork water was brackish and unsuitable for drinking and Elm Creek proved to be dry more often than not. An eighty-foot well was dug but found to be unreliable also. Later occupants of the fort succeeded in digging a well some twenty feet in diameter that held seven feet of water, but it is uncertain when this was accomplished.

Building materials were also a problem. Abercrombie was so appalled at the conditions, he tried to protest to General Smith that the site was unsuitable, but the general was on detached duty for several weeks and unavailable, so Abercrombie proceeded as ordered.[16] Perhaps if General Smith had been available, the post on the Brazos would never have been established.

After a plan for the design of the fort was laid out, the logs for building the officers quarters had to be hauled up to forty miles to the site in ox-drawn wagons. The other buildings were made of jacal construction consisting of upright staves chinked with mud.

The records do not indicate how the troops were housed during the construction of the fort's facilities, but it is likely they used their regular tents and bedding until the permanent construction was completed.

Clear Fork present day. Courtesy of Bill Wright, author.

Fortunately there was a good supply of stone that awaited a stonemason to use. When the stonemason, a civilian named Leanhardt, arrived at the scene, stone chimneys for the fireplaces were constructed. The magazine, guardhouse, and commissary were built entirely of stone. Other stonemasons mentioned in the official records were Valentine Leonard and Daniel Wilson, the guide, who doubled as Leonard's assistant as well as Maltby, the muleskinner.[17] Each of the stone masons received $45.00 per month.

Archaeologists have found that the remains of the earliest American lime kilns in west Texas were in association with Army forts built in the 1850s. In the case of Fort Phantom, four lime kiln ruins discovered on Elm Creek were probably used to produce the material that chinked the log barracks and produced the stonework for the post.[18]

Many of the frontier forts made provisions for the wives of the men. Although some of the officers later brought their wives to the post, Lear never did. His wife's home was in New Orleans and they spent Christmas there. Unfortunately, before Christmas, their infant son died and was buried in the cemetery at Fort Washita. Lear requested a six-month leave and on his return, brought library books for the post at the request of his friend, Lieutenant William Wallace Burns. Evidently Abercrombie was still attempting to move the post because Burns also reported to Lear that General Smith refused to consider moving the post.[19]

First Lieutenant Lear wrote his wife at Fort Washita to describe the actions and observations of the first few days in camp. At that point, the harshness of the west Texas landscape must have escaped him. Perhaps he wanted to assure her of his surroundings so that she would not worry. The first night, he described his first impressions of the site:

> Our destination has at length been reached, and too much cannot be said of its beauty, as far as view and magnificent valley are concerned, but the great disinclination, timber for building purposes is to all appearances at first glance, entirely wanting, there being no other than black jack or low scrub oak and not the greatest quantity of that.[20]

After a few days on the site, Lear began to think differently. On November 19, in another letter to his wife, he wrote:

> When I say to you that we have a beautiful valley to look upon, I have said everything favorable that could be said of this place. We are camped in a grove of blackjack two or three hundred yards of the creek which is salt, or brackish and bitter. A spring has been discovered ten miles off, which affords very little water. Everybody is disgusted. Like the Dove after the Deluge, not one green sprig can we find to indicate this was ever intended by man to inhabit. Indeed, I cannot imagine that God ever intended for white man to occupy such a barren waste.[21]

Mrs. Emma Johnson Elkins, in her recollections of Fort Phantom Hill as a young child living there with her father, an ordnance sergeant, described an eight-foot-wide trench constructed around the camp with the cannon placed in the center on a parapet. Elkins wrote that the northern Comanche Chief, Buffalo Hump, once came with his band with warriors, squaws, and children, numbering some 2,400 souls.[22] He frequented the area and was generally hostile to whites. Elkins, who was four years old at the time, possibly exaggerated the number of visitors.

A number of other details concerning the establishment of Fort Phantom were overlooked. In addition to the lack of water and construction materials the land on which the fort was built was not unclaimed. It was customary for speculators to file on land unseen in anticipation of resale or future use. Whiting and others already warned the War Department that steps should be taken to acquire the property on which the new forts were to be constructed but the recommendation was ignored. General Smith was also concerned with land ownership. In a letter to the Western Division, Smith "most earnestly" suggested the federal government get title to the land on which forts were to be built, observing that unless the government owned the land, as soon as the facility was constructed, the owner would immediately raise the rentals and fees for the timber and grass. Unfortunately, Smith's suggestion was also ignored.[23]

The land on which Fort Phantom was constructed was originally owned "as part of a head right grant acquired by William E. Evans from the Republic of Texas on June 29, 1838." In Jones County records, it is still shown on maps as the "Evans Survey." In 1841 it was deeded to Charles Chamberlain and, at his death, a Harris County Court sold the land at public auction. It was purchased by A. C. Dawson on August 3, 1851, for fifty dollars. It is interesting to note that this occurred three months before the arrival of Abercrombie at Phantom "Bluff."[24] One might wonder if Dawson had acquired prior knowledge of the future location, but Dawson probably had never seen the land he purchased because of its isolation. At the time, Dawson's ownership did not present a problem and there were only scattered Indian villages in the area. In addition to Fort Phantom, several of the new forts were constructed on land that had been surveyed or claimed before the time of construction.

The first civilian settlement in the area also began in November 1851, when Jesse Stem, an Indian agent, built a log cabin on what was later the famous Lambshead Ranch in present Throckmorton and Shackelford counties. His intention was to sell corn and beef to the forts at Phantom Hill, Belknap, and Chadbourne. His venture failed when he was murdered by Tonkawa Indians on February 12, 1854.[25]

Posts established in Texas between 1848 and 1852 shared important characteristics, although there were no standard plans. This was because of the mandate that utmost economy should be maintained throughout. Therefore, the construction of all the frontier forts was generally done by the troops themselves with little assistance from skilled craftsmen.[26]

Because Fort Phantom was constructed with as little direction as many of the frontier forts during the period between 1851 and 1854, the officers in the field used their individual judgment, taking into consideration availability of materials and local terrain. Fort Phantom was "home built" by the troops who established it.

Soon after construction was underway at Fort Phantom, Abercrombie and his men established a road to Fort Chadbourne, connecting the two posts through the Callahan Divide at Mountain Pass. They skirted Castle Peak, a prominent outlier of the Callahan Divide that could be seen for more than fifty miles at the

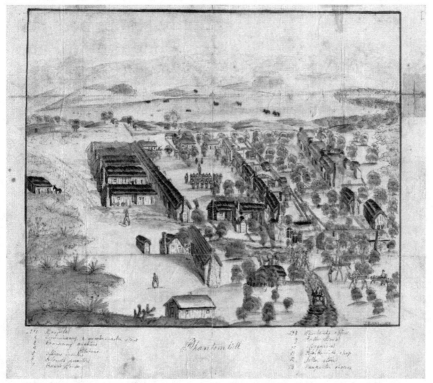

Fort Phantom. Courtesy of Center for American History. UT-Austin. Albert Sidney Burleson Papers. di-04124.

time. Early accounts refer to the landmark as "Abercrombie Peak," reflecting his account of the expedition.

The road was used infrequently throughout the early 1850s because the posts were supplied from other, more direct routes. Fort Phantom was supplied from the east and Fort Chadbourne from the southeast. The Marcy trail to the west was the route preferred by travelers enroute to El Paso.

Colonel William G. Freeman made an inspection tour of the Eighth Military Department in August 1853 and noted that there had been practically no communications between the two posts. Because of a lack of use, the trail was indistinct and difficult to follow. Lieutenant Richard Irving Dodge, stationed at Fort Chadbourne, made a sketch of the trail for Freeman but he still became lost en route to Fort Phantom, costing him half a day of travel.[27] Mrs. Elkins recalled camping overnight with her family on the road between the forts at the Mountain Pass in February 1854. At this time, Mrs. Elkins was a child about six years old, but she still remembered the events of that night.

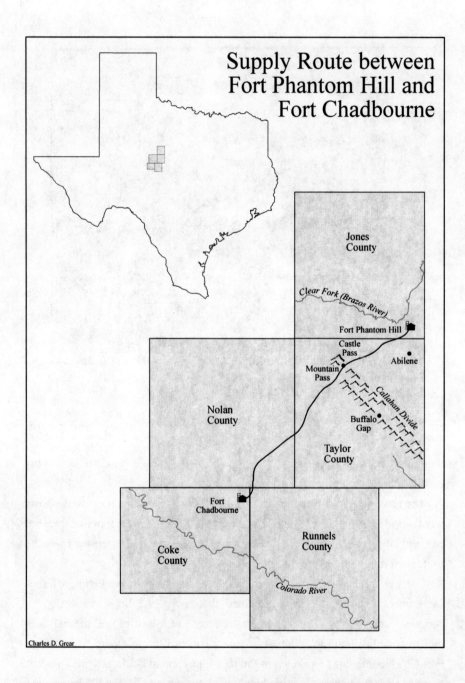

Supply Route between
Fort Phantom Hill and
Fort Chadbourne

Jones
County

Clear Fork (Brazos River)

Fort Phantom Hill

Castle
Pass

Mountain
Pass

Abilene

Callahan Divide

Nolan
County

Buffalo
Gap

Taylor
County

Fort
Chadbourne

Runnels
County

Coke
County

Colorado River

Charles D. Grear

We were enroute to [Fort Chadbourne] when Major Stemm [Stem] was murdered by Kickapoo Indians. When within 12 miles of our destination, and encamped in a gorge of the mountains which formed the chain in which Mountain Pass was situated, and just as the sun was setting, a rider appeared coming toward our camp, who proved to be Jim Shaw, the Delaware chief, who brought tidings of the killing of Major Stemm. On information of the murder reaching Phantom Hill, the old chief immediately mounted his horse and, alone, started in pursuit of us to warn us of danger. The chief remained in that camp that night never closing his eyes to sleep but sat up keeping watch. The next morning he bade us a kindly adieu and returned to his people.[28]

Smith's choice of the site known as Phantom Hill for a second post in the Brazos River region was not met with great enthusiasm by the officers of the Fifth Infantry, and until February 1852, they entertained some hopes it would be moved, preferably to the area Marcy and Belknap had recommended on Pecan Bayou. Initial dismay over the appearance of the Phantom Hill area was probably heightened by the severe cold and subsequent drought that characterized the winter, spring, and summer and by the distance of the new post from sources of supplies. Nonetheless, preparation of a site for the new fort went forward, and a significant amount of construction was completed between November 1851 and June 1852 without guidance from headquarters in San Antonio.

By early summer, the fort was enough of a permanent installation to encourage the confidence of potential settlers, and the land that surrounded the installation, as well as the one-third league on which it was located, was surveyed for private holders of certificates.

Reports from Phantom Hill during the early 1850s indicate that the site was not a particularly desirable one for a military installation despite its proximity to the Clear and Elm Forks of the Brazos River. The streams, which were an unreliable source of water during drought conditions, averaged thirty feet in width. In the immediate vicinity of the fort, the soil was poor and shallow. Cultivable areas were located at some distance, a distinct disadvantage in an area where only 9.44 inches of rain were reported during the first eight months of 1853. The grasses, which were necessary to feed the herds of cattle, horses, mules, and oxen were quickly depleted. Nor were the trees available in the vicinity appropriate for construction of a large, five-company post. The fort site was located in a five-acre grove of scrub oak. Trees available at a great distance included blackjack oak, elm, pecan, and hackberry. Freeman in his report cited the difficulty of obtaining wood and cited the water as "not good." He referred to the soil as fertile and the grass good.[29]

Surgeon Conally described the area in his later 1854 report on Texas forts, indicating little change in the characteristics of the land between Abercrombie's and Freeman's reports and his a few years later:

> This post was situated between the Clear and Elm forks of the Brazos River about a mile and a half above the point where they unite to form the main Clear fork. Their average width was about thirty feet and usually were fordable by a man on horseback without wetting his feet; but holes were very numerous where the water was much deeper.[30]

The post itself, Conally said, was situated in a grove of scrub oak about five acres in extent and surrounded by prairie. On the ridges and high ground the soil was poor and thin; but in the bottom, fair crops of corn could be grown.

The general character of the neighboring country was prairie. A few miles to the west was a thicket encompassing several miles that consisted of a low scrubby species of oak called "black-jack" with multitudes of green briars, which rendered it almost impenetrable. About thirty miles to the south was a small range of mountains dotted with a few groves of small timber mostly post oak and blackjack. Stunted mesquite trees were thinly scattered over the prairies, and a little timber consisting chiefly of elm, pecan, and hackberry, grew on the margins of the streams. The scarcity and character of the timber presented many obstacles to the erection of quarters, which were consequently a temporary construction.

The animals found near the post included the black bear, big white or grayish wolf, prairie wolf, panther, fox, fox squirrel, prairie dog, raccoon, skunk, jack rabbit, deer, and antelope. The rattlesnake and a long yellow snake called the prairie racer were abundant. Several species of the frog and lizard were plentiful. The rivers supplied the cat fish, mud cat, gar, sunfish, eel, bass, and "drum." Few bison had been seen in the vicinity since 1837.[31]

Fort Phantom Hill was never officially named as such. Called the "Post on the Clear Fork of the Brazos," it was known as Fort Phantom Hill for the hill on which it was located as reflected in the communications of General Smith, who established the location. The reasons for the name "Phantom Hill" are not known. There are several versions of the story: the one suggested by Major Abercrombie who led the detachment founding the camp; the recollection of Jeff Maltby, and another more mysterious version recounted by Emma Johnson Elkins in 1911. Her account stated that "On a bright moonlight night a group of officers and a party of men were encamped a short distance from the new post when one of the party saw a tall white figure on the hill." (Most likely an Indian with a white blanket.) One of the officers "suggests a name; we will call the fort 'Phantom Hill'. This name was unanimously adopted."[32]

The most logical reason for the name seems to be that, from a distance, the hill rises sharply from the plains but levels out as approached, disappearing as if a phantom. War Department records shed no additional information on the name, merely describing the location as the "Post on the Clear Fork of the Brazos" and that it was known locally as "Phantom Hill."[33]

5

Protecting the Frontier, 1851–1854

Life at Fort Phantom Hill quickly became routine, but it was difficult and lonely. The post was far from other locations and the men had few avenues for relaxation. Indians did not present a problem because their travels largely steered clear of the fort and those coming to the fort were not hostile. But there were difficulties.

As the post became fully staffed, it was manned by five companies of the Fifth Infantry: Companies C and G came with Major J. J. Abercrombie and two days later, Companies B, E, and K arrived. The initial roster detailed 231 men and fifty horses, and mules and oxen.[1] When additional troops arrived by April 1852, there were 284 officers and men, and the increased demand for food and shelter in the sparse environment created a severe strain on the available resources.[2] Compared to twenty-first-century temperatures, the climate was relatively mild. Temperature for August 1852 averaged a reasonable 79.7 degrees with only 0.03 inches of rainfall recorded.[3]

Health conditions at Fort Phantom, as with all the frontier posts, were problematic. The soldiers suffered from moldy supplies and the lack of fresh food. To counter this, the men gathered wild spring onions and wild plums though they did not last long. The assistant post surgeon, Alex B. Hasson, did all he could but, in addition to the injuries suffered in the normal course of life at a military post, disease also took its toll. Cases of consumption, rheumatism, and venereal disease were common. The childbirth deaths were more devastating than Indian attacks, he reported. During the long winter of 1852, one of Lieutenant William Wallace Burns' children died and was buried at Fort Phantom in a shallow grave. Hasson also reported various rattlesnake bites and one case of wild mushroom poisoning.

To counter these ailments, Hasson planted a garden, but it was not successful because of lack of rainfall. "We are told that more rain than usual has fallen," he wrote, reflecting that even in better times, the moisture was still woefully short. During 1852, Hasson reported that there were more men in the post hospital than the average monthly strength of the post. Most of the health problems were directly related to the poor quality diet and water. By July 14, cases of scurvy added to the problems related to diet and contributed to one death.[4]

Normally, the men could have been assured of a supply of fresh meat, but few buffalo had ranged that far south since 1837, perhaps because of climatic conditions. After the post was closed, ironically, they came back by the millions only to be slaughtered by commercial hunters.

Many of the problems of the health program reflected the problems of the army as a whole. Based on a largely nonscientific system of treatment and prevention, it was virtually guaranteed to fail.[5]

The soldiers did not suffer alone. Hasson noted that consumption, rheumatism, venereal disease, and childbirth defects were also devastating the Indian population.

Resupply and communication was difficult, and there was a need for constant contact between the officers at the fort and the various supply agencies of the government. Soon after the construction of the post began, Major Abercrombie set out to find a shorter route to Fort Belknap. The detail conducting the survey set out a new road that was about ten miles shorter, and it became the permanent military road.[6]

Conditions did not improve during the year. In a letter to Quartermaster General Thomas on December 22, 1852, Capt. Thomas F. Hunt in New Orleans reported on the delay in shipments from Preston on the Red River more than a year after the post was established. He cited the distance from Preston to Fort Belknap as being about 170 miles with an additional 70 miles to Fort Phantom. Many forts obtained their supplies primarily from San Antonio, whereas Fort Phantom Hill and other frontier forts occasionally transferred supplies among themselves as needed. This required an extensive network of independent teamsters. Some fifty-two wagons driven by these independents plied the route between Indianola on the coast to San Antonio, whereas seventy-two teams driven by the individual posts being supplied transferred supplies from San Antonio to the forts. The cost from San Antonio to Fort Chadbourne, some 230 miles, was approximately $1.43 per hundredweight.[7] In addition to the unpredictable supply, many of the items arrived spoiled or damaged. The route of supply was later changed.

In 1853, soldiers were moved to Fort Phantom Hill from Fort Gates, near present-day Gatesville, when the need for protection in that area diminished and the fort was abandoned. O. J. Tyler, who had a farm near Fort Gates, and Mr. Dalrymple contracted with Fort Phantom to supply feed for the livestock as they apparently were doing for Fort Gates. They employed a man named Deaton to transport the feed. For several years, Deaton made the journey of two hundred miles with his team of oxen and recalled there was not a single settlement along the way.

There were Indians, however, but they did not attack his wagons. Deaton wrote:

> One morning when the train moved out and while crossing a big ridge, we discovered a large body of Indians about one mile from us. Evidently their intention was to attack us, but everything was made ready and we moved on with our wagons in a double string and the Indians seeing that we were in good order, after coming near, drew off, but fired the prairie in order to harass us. The grass being very tall, it was difficult to keep it from consuming our wagons. They kept this up for several days, but we kept everything in order and were ready for an attack at any time. An Indian is not apt to make an attack unless he has the advantage, and the old bull drivers were not disposed to give any.[8]

Food shipped from Preston often spoiled before it arrived at the remote post. On September 3, 1853, First Lieutenant Burns wrote General John Gibbons concerning a shipment of spoiled food:

> September 3, 1853
> Phantom Hill, Letter to Bvt. Maj. Gen. Gov. (John?) Gibbons, Com. Gen. Subsistence, Washington from Wm. W. Burns, 1st Lt. 5' Infantry
>
> General,
>
> I was forced to present to a Board of Survey this day eighty-nine barrels of pork and thirty kegs of onion pickles, a part of the surplus sent via Red

River, Texas shipped in 1851, and some 9 months en route. I have kept those on hand as long as it was possible to issue them. Now they are totally spoiled, and four companies of the post are ordered to the Rio Grande.

The last lot condemned I reported impossible to sell but fortunately on the day of the sale a train of Public Wagons were here and I offered the Bidders permission to haul the provisions to Austin, Texas; and established the minimum price of flour at one dollar per sack, the bread at $1.25 per barrel, (sic). After the first two or three bids when I found them selling for almost nothing. This good fortune cannot happen to the stores now condemned.

I also presented 7 barrels of ham just rec'd and found to be entirely spoiled. I have now none but good provisions, except occasionally a bad barrel of flour on hand have just moved into a fine new commissary store.[9]

Burns was quite resourceful in making the most of a bad situation but that did not alleviate the problem. Food was difficult to supply within the far-flung network, and clothing and equipment were also scarce. Fort Phantom Hill had no standard for clothing. Regulation uniforms were impractical on the frontier. Many wore old Mexican War uniforms, and few had even a complete fitting of those.

When W. G. Freeman surveyed the western posts for the Eighth Infantry and made a report in the fall of 1853 on the status of the frontier forts, he stated the troops at Phantom Hill had only "fatigue clothing . . . [and] many of the recruits had not had their overalls and jackets altered to fit."[10]

If food and clothing were difficult, weapons for the troops presented an equally awkward problem. At Fort Phantom, Freeman found fifty-five men were without arms of any kind and others had what they could get.[11] Many had only the old 1842, .69-caliber smoothbore Springfield musket, which had been relatively unchanged for nearly one hundred years.

There was such difficulty with supply, that the Assistant Quartermaster, Bvt. Major W. W. Chapman, considered using the Rio Grande River as a transportation route. He ordered Capt. Harry Love to explore the river to see if steamers could supply the river forts that were presently supplied overland from Lavaca. It was an interesting idea but doomed to failure if attempted. As Mrs. Cazneau observed, the river had been at an unusually high level for around twenty years because of higher than usual rains upstream. The local tribes thought the arrival of the settlers and troops were responsible for the diminished water flow, and she berated the authorities for encouraging their superstitions.[12]

From the time of its establishment, there were rumors that the post was to be relocated, and the report made by Freeman also suggested that the fort would be better situated elsewhere because of the lack of available water and supplies. He thought the "aspect of the place [was] uninviting. No post visited except for Fort Ewell, presented so few attractions." Before visiting Phantom Hill he had inspected Fort McKavett and, afterward, Fort Chadbourne, ninety-five miles to the northwest of McKavett on Oak Creek, a small tributary of the Colorado.

At Fort Phantom Hill, he found conditions somewhat similar. Except for the officers, who lived in "two or three rude, 'jacal huts,'" the troops there were still living in tents." "The Comanches are the only Indians who have visited the post since its establishment," he wrote. "I could obtain only a vague estimate of their numbers. They have no permanent camps, but for the last year the band of San-a-co, one of the principal chiefs, has lived within fifty or sixty miles of the post."

Freeman could not review the troops because nearly all were raw, untrained recruits who had not yet learned even how to march. Adding to this dismal scene, he wrote, "The officers and soldiers are living in pole huts built in the early part of last year. They are now in a dilapidated condition. The company quarters will, in all probability, fall down during the prevalence of the severe northers of the coming winter."[13]

After inspecting Phantom Hill, he proceeded to Fort Belknap, on the Clear Fork of the Brazos where the prospects were brighter. There was plenty of good stone and brick clay for construction; the post stood over a field of bituminous coal that could be dug for fuel, and excellent springs were only a few hundred yards away.

The post had been visited recently by small bands of Caddos, Anadarkos, Ionies, Wacos, Keechies, and Tawakonis, as well as three hundred Comanches under the leadership of the ubiquitous Buffalo Hump and Sanaco. "Their camps are moveable," Freeman wrote, "but during the winter they live within forty miles, on the Clear Fork."

Freeman swung eastward from Belknap to a small collection of log buildings called Fort Worth at the mouth of the Clear Fork of the Trinity River. "The nearest towns or villages are Dallas, with 350 inhabitants, thirty-eight miles east, and Birdville and Alton, with a population of fifty each, and distant nine and thirty-five miles respectively."[14]

On April 27, 1852, Abercrombie turned the command of Fort Phantom Hill over to Lieutenant Colonel Carlos A. Waite, who was succeeded by Major Henry

Major Henry Hopkins Sibley. Courtesy of the Prints and Photographs Division, Library of Congress. Photo No. cwpb-05992.

Hopkins Sibley on September 24, a scant five months later. By this time four of the five original companies had been withdrawn and the remaining company reinforced by Company I of the Second Dragoons.

Sibley's reputation was not good, but in one of the few actions that took place from the fort, his Dragoons recovered some hostages.[15]

In contrast to those seen at other locations, the troops at Fort Phantom Hill saw few Indians. A group of Penateka Comanches led by the infamous Buffalo Hump continued their visits and caused no harm. Although they were regarded as potentially hostile, they did not engage the foot soldiers of the post on their home ground, weak as the defenses appeared. Mrs. Elkins noted that an eight-foot trench had been constructed around the fort for defensive purposes.[16]

Still, Buffalo Hump's visits were enough to make the troops at Fort Phantom nervous. As one of more fractious of the Comanche leaders, he vigorously protested the establishment of the post, feeling it was located too close to the Indian hunting grounds, and it could be used for an attack on the tribe. It was necessary for the Indian agent, Jessie Stem, to reassure Buffalo Hump and other chiefs that "'Father Washington' wanted peace and desired only to help his 'Indian Children.'"[17] Whiting recounted in his report to his superiors that the foot soldiers of the fort did not represent a threat to the mounted Comanches who were expert horsemen and could run their steeds in circles around the immobile infantry.

On March 26, 1854, Lieutenant Newton C. Givens took command of the post. Givens, a West Point graduate, served with distinction during the battle of Buena Vista in 1847. Previously stationed at the post in Burnet, Givens had been reassigned as quartermaster to another post. He attempted to save the government money by purchasing corn locally at a cheaper price than was charged the quartermaster general in San Antonio. Invoking the ire of his superiors, he was court-martialed. Givens fought back, was able to have his case reviewed, and presenting evidence of fraud in the procurement of supplies, was reinstated and given a promotion.[18]

Givens did not have the chance to serve as commander of the post for long. The environmental conditions remained grim. Water quality and availability of fresh vegetables continued to be uncertain. General Persifor F. Smith responded to the complaints of the troops and the report of Freeman regarding the suitability of the location and ordered the post abandoned and the troops reassigned. On November 4, 1853, a letter was received by General Smith from Samuel Cooper in regard to the closing of the post and the reassignment of the forces. He responded, affirming the suggestion that a new post be established on the Rio Grande River near Presidio Del Norte.[19]

The letter was followed by Special Orders No. 125 from General Smith authorizing the redistribution of troops and supplies from Phantom Hill, Fort Mason, and Fort Terrell, which were also to be abandoned. By this time the Indians were mostly located in the reservation near Fort Griffin and seemed to have ceased to be a problem in the local area. There were increasing troubles on the Rio Grande border resulting in the transfer of two companies, one to Eagle Pass and another, Company I, to Fort Chadbourne.[20]

Lieutenant Givens continued to command the remaining troops until Fort Phantom Hill, the Post on the Brazos, was abandoned on April 6. Evidently feeling great relief and the belief that any future assignment would be under better conditions, the troops marched out of the post. Later, the fort mysteriously burned to the ground. The only structures that remained standing were the chimneys and other stone structures. Some blamed the troops; other theories held that an irate officer's wife was responsible. Perhaps it was the remaining Indians in the area who always resented the presence of the fort. No one knows, but the evidence points to departing troops.

Mrs. Elkins related that the fire was set by a soldier named Scullion, who was Givens' Negro slave. A trial was held in Eagle Pass where the slave testified that Givens ordered him to burn the fort "so that no other soldiers would ever have to be stationed in such a forsaken spot." Scullion was duly convicted of arson. This story was repeated by W. L. Ormsby, the first westbound passenger on the Butterfield Overland Stage.[21]

As the orders came to abandon Fort Phantom there was an additional reason the post was not continued, it had no constituency. A substantial community that depended on the federal influx of funds never developed around Fort Phantom Hill. As with contemporary military installations, local citizens with political influence who relied on the economic impact of the federal installation could have rallied to its support and created a political argument for the post to remain active. It was not until years later that a small community developed around the former fort, then used for other purposes. It was too late to influence any federal funding coming to the area.

Local communities are not always successful in keeping the federal installations, as with Fort Davis that closed in 1891 despite the efforts of the locals. However, there are many instances where local efforts succeeded to preserve and expand the federal presence. Fort Worth, Fort Duncan, and Fort Bliss in El Paso remained active for many years after the original mission was no longer viable and, in the case of Fort Bliss, continues as a major military installation to this day.

The sad ending of the fort did not end its usefulness. Adventures lay ahead for the standing stones of old Fort Phantom.

6
Butterfield Days,
1855–1861

Four years after Lieutenant Newton C. Givens led the remaining troops from Fort Phantom Hill for the last time, the burned-out remains of the former military post embodied the "Phantom" appellation. Through droughts, winter winds, and summer heat, there were only occasional reported visitations. Perhaps only the spirits, cited by Mrs. Elkins, remained.

Curious Indians possibly wandered through the ruins, grateful that at least one unwelcome stake in the middle of their hunting grounds was abandoned and not likely to be revived. Others also came, briefly stopping by or camping amid the remaining stone chimneys and spun stories of times past around a campfire.

Colonel Albert Sidney Johnston stopped by on March 26, 1855, as he traveled from Fort Belknap to Fort Chadbourne, accompanied by his son, William Preston Johnston.

The younger man was apparently aware of the controversy that surrounded the original site selection as he observed that General Persifor F. Smith must have had a "Napoleonic intuition" when he chose such an inappropriate place. He commented that: "At a distance the white stone chimneys loom up like the monuments of some populous graveyard, or you might fancy them sheeted ghosts in the mist and gloom of a norther. The name Phantom Hill, if not applicable

Albert Sidney Johnston. Courtesy of the Prints and Photographs Division, Library of Congress; Photo no. LC-DIG-pga-04023.

at the time, seems to have been prophetic."[1]

The two men lingered for a while and then continued their journey. The stone monuments to a former time had made their impression.

In 1853, Jefferson Davis, then Secretary of War, requested, and Congress authorized, the establishment of two regiments of mounted troops, the First and Second US Cavalry. The Second, ordered to Texas in 1855, was commanded by Colonel Johnston with Lieutenant Colonel Robert E. Lee as second in command. "The regiment fought fifty-five engagements with hostile Indians from January, 1856 to February, 1861."[2]

Lee, often erroneously cited as assigned to Fort Phantom Hill, passed the fort on the morning of June 16, 1856, on a reconnaissance with the first squadron of the Second Cavalry from Camp Cooper, where he was actually stationed. Several Indian depredations were reported in the vicinity of Fort Chadbourne, probably led by Chief Sanaco. Lee was placed in command of a search for the instigator, which led him by the fort. Guided by Jim Shaw's Delaware Indian scouts, they made good time and continued on to Mountain Pass where they spent the night, traveling to Fort Chadbourne the next day.[3]

Lee gained familiarity with the region while searching for a site for a new fort in the area, which the War Department determined was needed. Because little was known of the territory from the existing maps, Lee made almost daily rides to survey for possible sites early in his assignment to Camp Cooper. Although it is not recorded, it is reasonable to assume that he also passed the deserted post during those investigations.[4]

According to a post return dated February 28, 1857, Lieutenant J. H. Reynolds and seventy-seven men camped overnight at the ruins en route from Fort Chadbourne to Camp Cooper, a march of almost five days.[5]

There must have been others who traveled the military road between Fort Chadbourne and Fort Belknap who did not record their impressions. Occasional immigrants traveling the military road toward California and military supply wagons, among others, probably passed by and wondered if the ruins were a sign of an Indian victory. In reality, the post on the Clear Fork of the Brazos, as a military post, had been defeated by personal arrogance and a relentless nature that had not yet been tamed by man's technology.

In 1858, the old post on the Clear Fork of the Brazos had a spark of new life. It became a part of the new desire for better communication and transportation between the eastern and western United States. With increased activity and development in California, there was a need to quickly move mail and people across the continent.

John Butterfield, who erected the first telegraph line between New York City and Buffalo, sought and was awarded a government contract to run a transcontinental stage and mail delivery service. The Southern Overland Mail would run from the Mississippi Valley to the Pacific coast. He was imminently qualified to implement a stage service. He had already built and managed several stagecoach lines and had even built the first steam railroad in Utica, New York.[6] The Southern Overland Mail service had two eastern terminals, St. Louis and Memphis, which merged at Fort Smith, Arkansas. Waterman L. Ormsby, a newspaper man, made the first transcontinental trip. He began the journey in St. Louis with the principal owner of the new service, Butterfield, who traveled only part of the way. Perhaps Ormsby was not an adventurous man, but with a reporter's curiosity and a nose for news, he was ready for a trip that promised adventure.

It was September 15, 1858, and the long-awaited inaugural mail service from Tipton, Missouri (a short train ride from St. Louis) to San Francisco would carry Ormsby to Fort Smith.[7] There they would join the southern route from Memphis for the 2,795-mile journey across the western lands to the coast. Beyond the Red River, the coaches would be mule-drawn "celerity wagons," rough riding but strong.[8] The nine-passenger wagon had a canvas top and leather straps instead of springs. It was drawn by mules that Indians were less tempted to steal than the treasured horses used with the Concord coaches. In addition, the Concord coach was easier to overturn on the more primitive roads across Texas, between El Paso and Fort Belknap, where many stretches were only recently hacked out of the wilderness by Butterfield's men.

The seats on the celerity wagon converted into a bed that enabled four to nine passengers to sleep during the night as the stage traveled night and day, stopping only to change teams or eat one of three meals a day.

Ormsby covered the trip for his newspaper, the *New York Herald*, and gave his readers a feel for crossing the wild and untamed west. The company's instructions for travelers suggested they travel armed in case of attack because the route through Texas, New Mexico, and Arizona crossed hostile Indian territory. Fortunately, over the entire life of the contract, the wagons were never attacked by Indians or renegades, although regular raids were made on the horse corrals to steal the valuable ponies. Perhaps Butterfield's decision to never carry payrolls or money deterred possible aggressors.

The contract won by Butterfield provided for twice weekly mail service to the west coast and back as far as St. Louis, Missouri, and Memphis, Tennessee. Butterfield proposed to make the trip in no less than twenty-five days and use four horse coaches to carry mail and passengers with the exception of the mules used with the celerity wagons. The southern route was chosen by the Postal Department even though it was somewhat longer than a middle route because the horses, mules, and wagons were not equipped for winter storms, which would block passage for months in the northern areas. In addition, the traffic developed by the Colorado Gold rush had, by 1859, when gold was discovered in Colorado, driven the Indians into a frenzy. In good weather, the Pony Express, which routed through the central part of the country worked well, but in the first test in the hard winter conditions of 1860–1861, they could not maintain a regular schedule and posted substantial delays. The Postmaster General, Aaron V. Brown, was correct when he favored the southern route of the Butterfield Overland Mail.

The selection of the southern route also benefited the War Department. The improved transportation between forts along the route meant that soldiers along the Texas frontier would have somewhat better living conditions because of easier supply delivery and communication. The travelers would also benefit from the additional protection afforded by the nearby troops.

The exact route grew from an 1854 survey by Captain John Pope as part of a national project carried out by the War Department titled "Explorations and Surveys for a Railroad route from the Mississippi River to the Pacific Ocean." After exiting Indian Territory, the route entered Texas at Colbert's ferry on the Red River. The twenty-five slaves of Chickasaw Indian Benjamin Franklin Colbert maintained the approach road and poled the ferry across the river. The road continued from

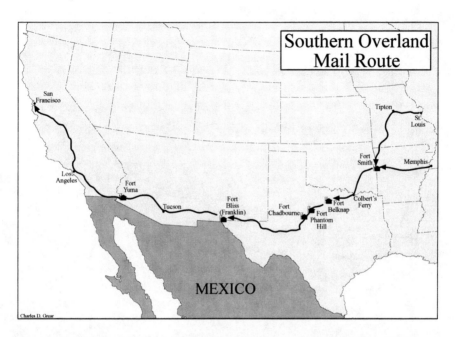

the crossing to Sherman, Gainesville, Fort Belknap, and the Clear Fork Station on the Brazos.[9] After fording the Clear Fork, the route continued to Phantom Hill and then headed southwest for sixteen miles, crossing the present I-20 to Mountain Pass and continuing twelve additional miles to Fort Chadbourne. From there the route continued past Grape Creek near the headwaters of the Concho River, where water was replentished for the dry seventy-mile traverse to the Horsehead Crossing. From there they traveled up the East side of the river to Pope's camp then following Delaware Creek to Delaware Springs and on to Hueco Tanks. From there it was but thirty miles on the Franklin (present-day El Paso). After resupply, the stages roughly followed the route of present I-10, and the east side of the Gila River to California, which became known as the "Gila Route."

In the arid sections of New Mexico Territory, the stations were spaced fifteen to twenty miles apart depending on the availability of water.[10]

As he mounted the coach that day in St. Louis, Ormsby had no idea the extent of the adventure he was undertaking, and he was also amazed at the general population's lack of excitement the prospect of a mail service to the west coast would provide.

"I looked forward in my imagination," he wrote that first morning, "to the time when . . . instead of having to wait over forty days for an answer from San Francisco, a delay of as many minutes will be looked upon as a gross imposition and of as many seconds a 'doing from fair to middling.'"[11]

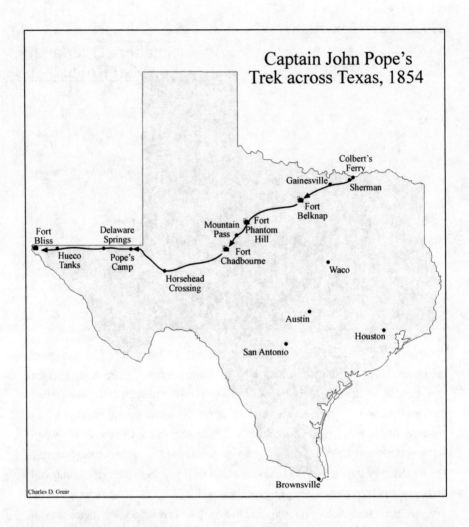

Captain John Pope's
Trek across Texas, 1854

Colbert's
Ferry

Gainesville

Sherman

Fort
Belknap

Mountain   Fort
Pass   Phantom
Hill

Fort
Bliss

Delaware
Springs

Fort
Chadbourne

Hueco
Tanks

Pope's
Camp

Horsehead
Crossing

Waco

Austin

Houston

San Antonio

Brownsville

Charles D. Grear

On the approach to Way Station 54, the stage crossed Dead Man's Creek, in eastern Jones County, which was named for James Moorehead who froze to death in the terrible blizzard that the men encountered near that location while en route with Colonel J. J. Abercrombie to establish the fort in 1851.[12]

By the time Ormsby arrived at Way Station 54 at Fort Phantom, he was already convinced of the rigors of the trip. Covered with dust from the coach's open windows, he stepped down to the welcome of Mr. and Mrs. Burlington.

> Mr. Burlington and his wife we found here all alone, hundreds of miles from any settlement, bravely stopping at their post, on Phantom Hill, fearless of the attacks of blood-thirsty Indians—as brave a man as ever

68

settled on a frontier, and a monument of shame to the cowardly soldiers who burned the post.[13]

The Way Station used three buildings that were not destroyed when the fort burned in 1854 as the federal troops departed. The magazine, which still stands, was used by the Butterfield mail agent Dr. Birch, as a storehouse. One of the other remaining structures that had stone walls became the station.

Ormsby referred to the station as "the cheapest and best station on the route" and observed that there was a fine well, eighty-feet deep and twenty feet in diameter that contained seventeen feet of water. Certainly an improvement over the privations the soldiers faced with the uncertain supply of water in the Clear Fork. He also had high praise for the Fort Phantom Hill stop observing: "Altogether, Phantom Hill is the cheapest and best new station on the route." Ormsby greatly admired the courage of Mr. and Mrs. Burlington.

> The station is directly in the trail of the Northern Comanches as they run down into Texas on their marauding expeditions. To leave this and other stations on the route so exposed is trifling with human life, and inviting an attack on the helpless defenders of the mail. As I have already said, there will be designing white men as well as Indians whose cupidity must be overawed by adequate military protection.[14]

Unfortunately, the fresh mules anticipated at the Fort Phantom Station were not there.[15] Ormsby and the stage were forced to continue toward the next stop at Mountain Pass.[16] Shortly before arriving at the Mountain Pass Station, they met a fresh team and proceeded to the station where they had breakfast.

Ormsby describes the breakfast as "coffee, tough beef, and butterless short cake, prepared by an old Negro woman, who, if cleanliness is next to godliness, would stand little chance of entering heaven."[17] There was an old saying, he said, that "every man must eat his peck of dirt." He felt he had done "good measure" to his peck on the trip.[18] Fortunately, the stage was not attacked by Indians during his trip.

Ormsby accompanied the coach to San Francisco to the post office where the first packet of mail was delivered at 7:30 a.m. on October 10, 1858, just twenty-three days and twenty-three and a half-hours after leaving Tipton. He had the additional satisfaction that he had set a new record—the first man to cross the plains in less than fifty days.[19]

* * *

In March 1861, the decision was made to modify the contract and establish a more direct route to the north, outside of Texas. The competitive Pony Express began in 1860, reducing the time of mail service to about ten days from St. Joseph, Missouri, to Sacramento, California. The Civil War also ended the Southern Overland Mail service. The Way Station of Fort Phantom Hill fell into disuse again.

The station at Fort Phantom was never attacked by Indians, although three men were killed at the station at Mountain Pass by fourteen Indians on April 12, 1860. James Hamby and Shadrach Styer were shot and scalped while walking some three hundred yards from the station house. Young William Lambshead, whose father, Thomas Lambshead was the manager at the next station at Valley Creek, was last seen running from the attackers and was never seen again and was presumed killed. Styer did not die immediately but crawled to the station entrance "scalped and dripping with gore, presenting a truly horrid appearance" but died shortly thereafter.[20] In addition, there were accidents. A soldier at the abandoned Fort Phantom Hill was shot by a resident who mistook him for a hostile Indian.[21]

The route of the stage as it crossed the future counties west of Belknap did not pass through any village or town, and with the exception of the village of Fort Phantom Hill that grew up around the old fort, never spawned a community as the area became occupied. The west Texas area it crossed remained lonely and sparsely populated for years to come.[22]

Ruins of Fort Phantom, Jones County, Texas. Courtesy of Bill Wright, author.

Ruins of Fort Phantom, Jones County, Texas. Courtesy of Bill Wright, author.

Ruins of Fort Phantom, Jones County, Texas. Courtesy of Bill Wright, author.

Fort Phantom Hill ruins. Photo courtesy of Southwest Collection/Special Collections
Library, Texas Tech Library, Lubbock, Texas, #SWCPC9 (B) – E11 #6 Texas Tech.

Chimneys at Fort Phantom. Photo courtesy of Abilene Photograph Collection, Hardin-Simmons University, Richardson Library, Abilene Texas. Photo # HSU81-01320.15c.

Chimneys before stabilization. Photo courtesy of Abilene Photograph Collection, Hardin-Simmons University, Richardson Library, Abilene Texas. Photo # HSU81-01320.15.

Store Building. Fort Phantom Hill around 1898. Photo courtesy of Abilene Photograph Collection, Hardin-Simmons University, Richardson Library, Abilene Texas. Photo # HSU90.06222-091.

Chimneys. Ruins of Fort Phantom Hill in 1948. Photo courtesy of Abilene Photograph Collection, Hardin-Simmons University, Richardson Library, Abilene Texas. Photo # HSU87-05119105a.

Front of powder magazine. Center for American History-UT Austin. Tualman (Joseph E.) Papers. di_03988.

Back of powder magazine. Center for American History-UT Austin. Tualman (Joseph E.) Papers. di_03990

People in front of powder magazine. Center for American History-UT Austin. Webb (Walter Prescott) Papers. di_04049.

Fort Phantom Hill ruins. Photo courtesy of Southwest Collection/Special Collections Library, Texas Tech Library, Lubbock, Texas, #SWCPC9 (B) – E11 #1Texas Tech; CC Rister.

Fort Phantom Hill ruins. Photo courtesy of Southwest Collection/Special Collections Library, Texas Tech Library, Lubbock, Texas, #SWCPC9 (B) – E11 #2 Texas Tech; CC Rister.

Fort Phantom Hill ruins. Photo courtesy of Southwest Collection/Special Collections Library, Texas Tech Library, Lubbock, Texas, #SWCPC9 (B) – E11 #3 Texas Tech.

Fort Phantom Hill ruins. Photo courtesy of Southwest Collection/Special Collections Library, Texas Tech Library, Lubbock, Texas, #SWCPC9 (B) – E11 #5 Texas Tech.

7

The Civil War, 1861–1865

Along the frontier in 1860, concerns were largely about defense problems, and national events were concerns of those in the settled areas where politicians and business people discussed the gathering tension between the Southern and Northern states. The industrialized North with a different way of life had become a threat to the agricultural South. Centered in the midst of this threat was the issue of slavery. Whereas the Northerners tended toward considering slavery a moral issue, those large landowners in the South felt it was their constitutional right to private property and that great economic loss would occur should they be freed. Along with the financial loss was the realization that the social structure of the South would be transformed by the advent of industrialization supplanting their way of life.

The two approaches to dealing with the thousands of slaves in the United States and the potential importation of more were deadlocked, and neither the North nor the South would budge. Historian T. R. Fehrenbach observed: "The essence of English-speaking politics, as more than one foreign observer has noted, depends on no one side or faction taking stands that may not or cannot, be compromised by rational man."[1]

So political action was doomed to failure and the nation prepared for war. The South understood they were losing control of the political situation in Washington and the feeling was they should just "get out of the union." It was a popular opinion and was held by the most prominent and active members of Southern society—the lawyers and politicians.

Texas Governor Sam Houston did not support secession and declined to call a convention to discuss withdrawal after South Carolina formally seceded from the union on December 20, 1860. Mounting political pressures caused a state convention to be called unconstitutionally and even Houston's reputation and stature could not keep the delegates from voting to secede on February 1, 1861. Even before the legislature legalized the action, there was movement to accept the surrender of federal forces in Texas.

At the time there were some two thousand federal forces in Texas, mostly scattered among the frontier forts with only two hundred or so at the headquarters of the US Army commander for Texas, Major General David E. Twiggs, in San Antonio. Twiggs, being a Southerner with strong sympathies for the Southern cause, sent repeated queries to Washington to ask for direction but received no response. Finally recognizing that bloodshed that would accompany resistance, and with the stars and stripes being torn down across the state and replaced with the emblem of a single star, he surrendered the federal establishment in Texas and along with them, more than $3 million of military supplies. At the time, this represented 10 percent of the US Army. Finally, the War Department chose to replace him with Colonel Carlos A. Waite, who was unable to alter the agreement made between Twiggs and the Texans. The military presence in Texas was transferred to the Confederate forces.

In the spring of 1861, most of the federal forces left Texas. Many of the frontiersmen were glad to see them go because of their inability to control the Indian raids and protect the extended settlements along the frontier. The departure of federal forces, however, necessitated a revised plan for the protection of the western frontier, which had suddenly become vulnerable.

Since before the days of the Republic, the frontier was protected by groups of volunteers called "Rangers" who were basically militiamen, raised from local communities when needed. These Rangers were officially recognized and received legal status in 1835 when a council met in San Felipe de Austin to manage the rising conflict with Mexico. On November 1 of that year, they commissioned a small group of twenty men to protect the frontier.[2]

As Texas moved into the Civil War, frontier troubles increased. After 1863, unlike other areas of the country, the settlers on the western frontier of Texas needed protection not only against the Indians but also the motley crew of deserters, draft dodgers, outlaws, and other disreputable types who helped make up the forces defending the rather porous areas between the frontier and settled areas of eastern Texas. They were called by many names: Minutemen, Texas Mounted Rifles, Frontier Regiment, or Border Regiment.[3]

After statehood and the Mexican War, the federal government had assumed responsibility for this protection and the Ranger organization was only used by direction of the governor on special occasions. The results had not been satisfactory because the frontier communities' Indian problems continued to escalate. Now with federal forces leaving, the officials of the state and Confederacy regained that responsibility.

The ruins of Fort Phantom Hill fell into the northwest district of the new Confederate military alignment that included Fort Chadbourne, Camp Cooper, and north to the Red River. Colonel Henry E. McCulloch was in charge and later, his command was extended south to the Rio Grande. At Camp Cooper on February 25, 1861, Colonel W. C. Dalrymple, commanding a Ranger company, accepted the unofficial surrender of the federal garrison from Captain S. D. Carpenter[4] and McCulloch traveled from his Confederate post at Camp Colorado, by way of Fort Phantom, to make the surrender official.

Recognizing the need for troops on the frontier after the departure of federal forces, the Confederate Secretary of War, H. P. Walker, authorized the organization of the First Regiment of the Texas Mounted Rifles. McCulloch placed the former Texas Ranger, Major James B. (Buck) Barry, in command of forces at Camp Cooper. On March of 1861, Barry extended his forces by sending Company H of the Texas Mounted Rifles to staff an outpost at the abandoned Fort Phantom Hill and placed Captain Milton Boggess in charge of the detail at Phantom Hill. Boggess and his men were soon called to Camp Colorado along with other troops from Camp Cooper and Forts Chadbourne and Concho, for a major campaign against the Comanches.

The campaign was authorized by Regimental Orders No. 17 from headquarters of the First Texas Mounted Rifles at Camp Colorado, Texas, on August 6, 1861. These orders instructed the troops from Forts Concho and Chadbourne and Camp Colorado to depart on September 1, and for those from Fort Phantom and Camp Cooper to depart on September 12. Troops from Camp Jackson were to deploy on September 15. Each man was to carry sixty days of rations and one hundred rounds of ammunition.

The orders specified that there would be one wagon for every fifty men and ten pack mules would be used to transport the provisions and ammunitions. Every man was to be prepared in every respect, with horses shod and arms in order with plans to be away from the post for the sixty days.

The campaign against the Comanches was a great success and, for some time until the frontier forces were withdrawn to other areas for battles against Union forces outside of Texas, the area was relatively quiet. Major Barry moved from Camp Cooper to Fort Belknap during this time and various units encamped at Phantom Hill while pursuing renegades of one stripe or another, but sorties were basically ineffective in controlling the Indian population that moved eastward again to fill the vacuum left by the absence of the federal forces.

Company H of the Frontier Regiment camped at Phantom Hill periodically between 1863 and 1864, but by 1865 the frontier defense system had essentially collapsed. Most of the frontier was without forces able to control the lawlessness of renegade whites, deserters, Indians, and miscellaneous outlaws.

As a result of the increased predation from Indians and the unsafe travel, the settlers on the frontier moved back toward the interior of Texas or "forted up" in private encampments for mutual protection. Many settlers migrated out of Texas altogether and made a new life in California or other western areas.

Samuel P. Newcomb and his family joined several other area families and forted up near the abandoned Fort Phantom, on the northeast bank of the Clear Fork of the Brazos at the location of the Johnson Ranch headquarters that previously had been burned by the Comanches. The settlers hoped this location, about fifteen miles south of Camp Cooper, would serve as protection from the Indians. The group began construction of a picket stockade on October 20, 1864, and soon afterward moved into their meager picket houses, covered and chinked with dirt. Shortly before, there had been an Indian raid on families who had settled near Elm Creek at its junction with the Brazos River. It was obvious the threat was increasing, but Newcomb and his new bride resolved to stay as long as possible near their land.

On January 1 of the next year, Newcomb resolved to begin a diary and continue it each day. His first journal entry described the situation they faced: "For the past year," he wrote, "they (the Indians) have been so troublesome and ha(ve) come down upon us in such large bodies that a great many of the old settlers have left the frontier and mov(ed) to older settled countries where Indian depreda(tions) are unknown."[5]

This diary recounted the controversial battle between Confederate forces and their state militiamen allies with a large encampment of Kickapoo Indians. The Indian's abandoned camp had been discovered in early December about thirty miles up the Clear Fork from the ruins of Fort Phantom. On January 8, 1865, Confederate soldiers located and attacked the encampment of the Kickapoos at Dove Creek, about twenty miles southwest of present-day San Angelo. The Kickapoos, who were totally peaceful and who were migrating to Mexico from Indian territory, prevailed in the battle and continued their way to sanctuary in Mexico. As a result of the unprovoked attack, the Mexican branch of the Kickapoo tribes began a series of attacks on frontier settlements that amounted to an all-out war against settlers along the border. In 1873, an invasion of Mexico by Colonel Ranald S. Mackenzie put an end to the attacks.[6] Later in his journal, Newcomb described hunting buffalo that had returned to the area after an absence of several years. Unfortunately, Newcomb did not survive until order could be restored to the frontier and his journal was continued by his widow as she faced life alone with a small child.

8
Fort Griffin Days, 1865–1872

The Civil War slowly came to an end in the spring of 1865, beginning with Robert E. Lee's surrender at Appomattox Court House and continuing as other Confederate forces gave up after hearing that news. On June 19, 1865, federal troops formally returned to Texas.

Soon after the final surrender of the remaining Confederate troops in April and May of 1865, the federal presence returned to the western frontier of Texas. The second line of forts was strengthened by the addition of two additional facilities: Fort Davis in the Big Bend area and Fort Stockton, both protecting the military road that led from San Antonio to El Paso.

Along with the federal troops, came the frontier cattlemen, many of them former Confederates, returned after the war to reestablish their ranches and reunite with their families. The times were turbulent. While the ranchers were at war, there were few men to care for the cattle herds, mixing on the open range and running wild across the prairie. The frontier tradition had always been for cattlemen to round up the free-ranging cattle and brand the calves with the brand of the mother. As they moved, the herd they would drop off a neighbor's branded cattle on their spread. Whereas the cattlemen were away fighting, unscrupulous men often stole the loose animals for their own. The returning cattlemen found

Charles Goodnight. Courtesy of the Armstrong County Museum, Claude, Texas.

that their herds had substantially diminished during their absence.

Charles Goodnight, a thirty-five-year old who served as a frontier ranger with Major Buck Barry at Fort Belknap, established a ranch in the area, but because of constant Indian attacks and thieving whites, he decided to gather a herd and drive it to New Mexico where the animals would be sold at Fort Sumner. With his experience as a Ranger during the war, and being familiar with the territory west of the second line of forts, he considered driving the herd straight across the Southern plains to New Mexico. However, he also was aware of the potential for constant battles with the Comanches and Kiowas who still held much of that country.

After more consideration, Goodnight decided the safest route would be the old Butterfield Southern Overland Mail trail through Camp Cooper, passing the abandoned chimneys of Fort Phantom Hill and the site of present-day Abilene. From that point, because of an easier terrain for cattle, he chose the alternate Buffalo Gap route of the Overland Mail to Fort Chadbourne; the route continued past present-day San Angelo, following the Middle Concho River westward. At the Middle Concho's headwaters, the trail headed into Centralia Draw, crossing the waterless barren desert to the Horsehead Crossing of the Pecos River and then to New Mexico. The route was longer but skirted the territory most likely to be attacked by Indians. Scarce water made the route equally dangerous for men and animals, not to mention the possibility of transient Indians from the plains traveling south to raid the prosperous ranches of northern Chihuahua.[1] On June 6, 1866, the drive commenced, history was made, and old Fort Phantom shared the passing glance of another man whose name would grace the history of the state.

Horsehead Crossing Marker. Courtesy of Bill Wright, author.

During the ten years between 1865 and 1875, many groups who followed the pioneering Goodnight and Oliver Loving, were harassed by the ever-present Comanches. Historian J. Evetts Haley observed that:

> [E]very man who drove was in danger of losing his cattle and having his "hair lifted" besides.—All along the trail were graves, now in forgotten places and holding forgotten men. W. H. Boyd, veteran of the drive of 1867, recalls many fresh mounds that "had never been rained upon." Astraddle of one near Fort Phantom Hill was a brand-new cowboy's saddle, both shelter and marker for the owner who slept beneath.[2]

In 1867 the army established Fort Griffin in Shackelford County. The older posts of Belknap, Chadbourne, and a reoccupied Fort Phantom Hill became subposts.[3] At the same time, units of the Ninth Cavalry were moved to Fort Davis and Fort Stockton to protect the stage route between El Paso and San Antonio. The entire western area was awash with various Indian groups that had run free during the years of the Civil War and were raiding the returning settlers with impunity. In addition, the sporadic internal wars in Mexico gave birth to an unprecedented lawlessness with bandits and bands of would-be revolutionaries crossing the border and joining with white outlaws, increasing the problems of the military. Adding to their problems was the illegal trade in stolen goods and cattle by the Comancheros—mostly Hispanic New Mexicans who traded with the Indians for their stolen goods. They took the goods and sold them back to the army and other settlers in New Mexico. The worrisome Comanches were among their better customers.

In his annual report for 1867, the Superintendent of Indian Affairs for New Mexico wrote the territory "was filled with Texas cattle."[4] The commanders in Washington either did not believe the conditions were as bad as they were reported or, for other reasons, were reluctant to do anything about it. Many more troops were needed to control the area than Washington had seen fit to provide because troops were needed in many other places during the turbulent days of Reconstruction and were not available for the frontier.[5]

The problems were so widespread and army support so thin, the men of the Ninth Cavalry at Fort Concho who were stationed south of the former post at Phantom Hill covered thousands of miles of arid territory and rode their horses to near exhaustion. At the same time, the Indians continued to be elusive and difficult to contain or confront. Finally, troops at Fort Concho had some success.

In September of 1869, a war party of Comanches and Kiowas attacked several locations near Fort McKavett and headed north toward their reservation on the Clear Fork near Camp Cooper. Captains Henry Carroll and Edward Heyl accompanied by ninety-five men took up the chase. They caught up with the Indians camped near the headwaters of the Salt Fork of the Brazos and immediately attacked, chasing the panicked Indians until their tired horses began to fail.

Encouraged by Carroll's success, Captain John Bacon led a detachment from Fort Concho northward, camping at the site of old Fort Phantom Hill. There he joined men from the Fourth Cavalry and some Tonkawa Indian scouts and moved up river and camped. At sunrise, more than five hundred Indians attacked from all sides and the fighting was fierce. After a protracted struggle, which at times was hand to hand, the Indians fled. Bacon followed them and on October 29 attacked their camp, killing forty and taking women and horses captive.[6]

Small garrisons from Fort Griffin were stationed at Fort Phantom and rotated each month. Each group consisted of a corporal and five to seven men. Their main job was to protect the new mail route that had been reestablished after the war through Mountain Pass to Fort Chadbourne, which connected the frontier forts with mail and passenger service.[7] The men made their camp near the ruins of the old fort and were able to get water from a sixty-foot well that they believed was dug by the previous soldiers or during the time that it was used by the Butterfield

Overland Mail. This provided a more dependable source of water than the intermittent nearby spring. Unfortunately in 1871, the wooden platform at the top of the well collapsed, rotted in the water below, making the water unfit to drink. Water again became a problem for the occupants of the former fort.[8]

In April of 1871, Colonel Ranald S. Mackenzie passed through the camp and described it as consisting of well-built chimneys and quarters for about five or six companies.[9]

The following month General William Tecumseh Sherman, General-in-Chief of the Army, made an inspection trip through the Fort Phantom area because of the increasing reports of Indian attacks. Randolph Marcy, who by this time had attained the rank of brigadier general and the post of inspector general, accompanied the group, and they camped overnight at Fort Phantom Hill. Marcy wrote in his journal "woodland was very scarce." As they traveled along the road from Fort Phantom to Fort Griffin, they noticed many signs of Indians and that many of the ranches were abandoned. He noted that there were not as many persons in the area as when

Ranald Mackenzie. Courtesy of the Prints and Photographs Division, Library of Congress; Photo no. 20540 USA; LC-USZ62-77935.

William Tecumseh Sherman. Courtesy of the Prints and Photographs Division, Library of Congress; Photo No. LC-B813- 6534 A [P&P].

he had visited eighteen years before and suggested, "If the Indian marauders are not punished, the whole country seems to be in a fair way of becoming totally de-populated."[10] However, by July the orders were given to discontinue the subpost, and all government property was returned to Fort Griffin.[11]

During the short period of activation, soldiers were sent from the encampment into the surrounding territory in search of Indians but no battles were recorded. During those two months, the soldiers made some improvement in the camp to deal with the summer heat but their efforts made no permanent impact on the facilities.

From August through December of 1871, a small detail was posted monthly at the location, but evidently the Indians were quiet and the cattlemen began moving back into the area. C. W. Merchant and others camped at Fort Phantom over the winter of 1871.

Joe McCombs, a young man of seventeen in 1871, related one account of the times. Striking out for himself, he took a job hunting the cattle that ran wild in the sand hills of Eastland County east of Fort Phantom Hill. He observed that his group of six or seven men were not bothered by Indians on the way north. They intended to drive the cattle all the way to Colorado but, when a chance came to sell them in Caldwell, Kansas, they were sold, perhaps because they were so unruly and wild that the constant stampedes along the drive were time consuming and dangerous. Returning to Texas, the men passed though the Comanche Strip and encountered Comanche warriors who surrounded them and relieved them of their supplies and tobacco but did not harm them.[12]

Unable to find work at his home in Desdemona, McCombs and a friend set out for Fort Griffin, located on a hill overlooking the Clear Fork. He recalled that in the flat below the fort, there was a small community that was a trading center for the fort and surrounding settlements. There were three saloons and three stores at the time.

The few ranches in the area were operated by George Greer and J. C. Lynch on Hubbard Creek, twenty-five or more miles south to southeast; Joe Browning was below Fort Davis on the Clear Fork, and Uncle Joe Matthews on the Clear Fork just below Griffin. John Larn was at the mouth of Tecumseh, and Mart Hoover at what is now known as the old Stone Ranch on Walnut Creek, then the farthest ranch house west in all this section. Judge Ledbetter was a few miles north of Fort Griffin and judge Stribling was in the Lamb's Head Valley above Fort Griffin.[13]

McCombs and his friend failed to find work at Fort Griffin and decided to return to San Antonio, but during the night before they were to leave and while

Fort Griffin, Officer's Quarters. From the Collection of the Robert E. Nail, Jr. Archives of the Old Jail Art Center, Albany, TX. FG (M) 0030.

Fort Griffin, Settler's Store. From the Collection of the Robert E. Nail, Jr. Archives of the Old Jail Art Center, Albany, TX. FG (M) 0050.

Fort Griffin, Bakery. From the Collection of the Robert E. Nail, Jr. Archives of the Old Jail Art Center, Albany, TX. FG (M) 0056.

Fort Griffin, Administration. From the Collection of the Robert E. Nail, Jr. Archives of the Old Jail Art Center, Albany, TX. FG (M) 0014.

Fort Griffin, Saloon. Courtesy of Bill Wright, author.

Fort Griffin, Saloon and Armory. Courtesy of Bill Wright, author.

camped a short distance from the town, Comanches stormed through with a herd of stolen horses. The two men were not harmed but their horses were taken. The next morning they reported the incident to Lieutenant Colonel George P. Buell at the fort and soon a scouting force followed their trail. The soldiers engaged the Indians but were forced back. Buell requested the assistance of Colonel

Fort Griffin, House. Courtesy of Bill Wright, author.

Mackenzie, who obtained a historic victory over the Comanches and secured the return of fifteen of the stolen horses, including that of McCombs' friend.[14]

By April of that year, the military commanders changed their minds yet again and reestablished Fort Phantom as a subpost of Fort Griffin, returning the equipment and tents used during the previous period and manning it with troops from Companies A, F, and G, of the Eleventh Infantry and Companies D and H, of the Fourth Cavalry.

In 1873 times were relatively peaceful because the year before, the Fourth Cavalry, led by Mackenzie, dealt a mighty blow to the Kwahadi Comanches gathered on the Staked Plains, capturing more than a hundred of their women and children, holding them hostage in the reservation to ensure peaceful behavior of the tribes. It would not last.

Lieutenant William Foulk, a troublemaking and disliked officer who had been promoted to command the "Buffalo Soldiers" of D Company of the Ninth Cavalry,[15] was sent to Fort Griffin, along with his equally troublemaking family.[16] The buffalo soldiers were not always well received by local populations, but they were good fighters, and their units, although generally supplied with inferior equipment, accorded themselves well in combat and military discipline. In the community that grew up around Fort Griffin as around Forts Richardson and Concho, that discipline was severely strained by the local population of drifters,

Old Stone Ranch, Two Buildings and Marker. Courtesy of Bill Wright, author.

Old Stone Ranch, Building and Stone Fence, Courtesy of Bill Wright, author.

prostitutes, thieves, and other unruly civilians. The post surgeon at Fort Griffin remarked, "When payday came, the killings would occur."[17]

Although much of the military action at the time centered at Fort Griffin and Camp Cooper, a new activity was soon to take place among the ruins of Fort Phantom Hill. The buffalo that had drifted away in the early 1850s when they were sorely needed for food by the founders of Fort Phantom Hill returned by the thousands. Men who discovered the value of their hides came with them.

The Buffalo Hunters, 1871–1883

When surveyors for the railroads began traversing the western frontier, it signaled the end of the need to protect the mail stages and launched the area into a new economic activity—hunting buffalo. Historian Wayne Gard observed:

> Although the hunting of buffalos was brief, it began after tanners learned how to make good leather from buffalo skins. It lasted only a dozen years, 1871–1883, seldom more than four years in any given section of the plains, yet that was enough to slaughter the enormous herds that had darkened the broad grazing lands of the west and virtually to wipe out the species. The killing left the prairies whitened with bones that pioneer farmers in need of a few dollars would pick up and haul to the nearest railroad town.[1]

Perhaps in the final analysis, it was the buffalo hunter who finally made the plains safe for the immigrants. He eliminated the primary food source for the Indians and effectively starved them into submission. This strategy was proposed by General William Tecumseh Sherman as part of his "final solution" of the Plains Indian "problem."[2]

Sherman felt that because "the inferior Indians refused to step aside so superior American culture could create success and progress, they had to be driven out of

101

the way as the Confederates had been driven back into the Union." As Sherman observed: "If there were no longer any buffalo near where the railroad traveled then the Indians would not go there either."[3]

Although Sherman's troops did not implement the policy, it was well executed by a ragged, adventurous mélange of men called "the buffalo hunters." After a dozen years of hunting by men like Wright Mooar and his compatriots, the buffalo were essentially eliminated from the landscape.

In 1871, there were millions of bison. In that year a giant herd estimated to consist of more than four million animals, stretching fifty miles deep and twenty-five miles wide was spotted near the Arkansas River in southern Kansas. Adventurers with the new deadly accurate .50-caliber Sharps rifles came to the buffalo country in droves to harvest the animals in what was to become the greatest massacre of warm-blooded animals in human history.[4] After the herds were thinned in Kansas, the hunters moved south to the Texas Panhandle and Rolling Plains.

At the beginning of the great buffalo hunt in Texas, the country west of Fort Griffin was still largely vacant. John Edward Elgin, a surveyor for the Houston & Texas Central Railway Company, in his testimony in the *State of Texas v. F. P. Olcott et al.*, describes the territory west of the Colorado in 1873:

> We had five ox wagons, several burros and thirty-three men, some mounted, some on foot. There were no settlements west of Camp Colorado in Coleman County, no road except [to] the old abandoned post of Ft. Chadbourne. We traveled . . . with little difficulty except at the creeks, where we had to make our own crossings. Horses, burros, and wagons were the only means of transportation at that time.

His observations regarding the nature of the country differ from its character today. Where once the country was generally expanses of grassy prairie, with scattered brush and mesquite mostly in the draws and creeks, today it presents a far different appearance being bisected by fences, roads, and ranch buildings.

After a month of travel, the group arrived at the last settlement on the Pacific Road, which was on Hubbard Creek. There was an abundance of buffalo and wild mustang horses but no cattle as far west as Phantom Hill or the present site of Abilene. The group encountered the last white man as they passed through Camp Colorado and the first woman on their return at Fort Griffin. Elgin remarked, "There were a good many Indians in the country, from whom we were not inclined to seek information."[5]

Much of the land on which the buffalo roamed and were hunted was purchased by speculators. In 1874, the state legislature began awarding tracts of land in the frontier portions of the state to charities and other special interests in lieu of cash to fund their activities. Cornelius Stribling and George A. Kirkland were hired by Houstonian W. R. Baker to sell the land on which Fort Phantom was built. Baker had acquired the land without ever venturing west to view the purchase.[6]

Presumably, the hunters did not bother to ask permission. They came by the hundreds and killed buffalo by the thousands. While working on a railroad survey crew, young Joe McCombs saw a large herd of some fifty thousand buffalo and returned on December 25 of 1874 to lead the first hunting expedition out of Fort Griffin. By the time he arrived, the buffalo had moved further south again, but despite that, he killed more than seven hundred buffalo in two months, taking the hides back to the fort to be shipped to tanners in the east. Then the party headed west toward Fort Phantom.[7]

West of Fort Phantom they encountered more buffalo and stayed out until the first of May. By the end of the season, they had secured more than 1,300 hides for which they received $2 each for the better, robe-grade hides and $1.50 for those of lesser quality. This batch of hides was the first significant number of pelts sold at Fort Griffin.[8]

Although the Indian "problem" seemed to be diminishing, there were still conflicts. Public opinion in settled areas was mostly on the side of the settlers. A typical opinion was expressed in the Fort Worth newspaper of September, 1873 when two of the principal chiefs were to be released from federal prison. The writer opined that the two would leave Fort Gibson where they were being kept and taken to Fort Sill where they would then be released on the reservation where they would continue scalping defenseless women and children and burn a few more wagons.

> Look at this matter in a legal constitutional light. These Indians committed several brutal murders within the jurisdiction of the State of Texas. They tied the poor wagoners to the wagon wheels and burned them slowly to death. The were tried, convicted and sentanced to be hung. But Davis at the request of the Washington government, that had no business or right to interfere, commuted their punishment to confinement, in the Penitentiary for life. Now the general government demands that they shall be pardoned and given up.[9]

This action resonated far beyond the state of Texas. Even in the distant state of Maine the *Springfield Republican* newspaper reported plans to release the two prisoners.[10]

In the fall of 1874, the Comanches were driven from their camp in Palo Duro Canyon near present-day Amarillo. Colonel Ranald S. Mackenzie's troops accomplished something even more important—they captured the Indian horses, rendering them unable to mount their attacks on settlers and travelers. This important raid and its success initiated what has been named "the Red River War" that largely eliminated Indian depredations in western Texas. The buffalo hunters were the beneficiaries of this and could pursue their acquisition of hides without harassment. Before the Red River War, it had been far more dangerous.[11]

The reputation of the Comanches lingered. When Mooar and his family made their way to Fort Griffin to hunt in the spring of 1875, they steered clear of the traditional Comanche haunts, traveling in an arc to the east and entering Texas through Forts Gibson and Denison where they added more wagons and traversed the old Butterfield Trail into Fort Griffin.[12] They were followed by many other groups that spread out in western Texas beyond Fort Phantom to Rath City and on toward present-day Midland. Buffalo hunting had become a serious enterprise.[13]

By the summer of the next year, Mooar, his brother John, and his group moved west, beyond Fort Phantom to an area near present-day Sweetwater in Nolan County where they found plenty of grass and water and hundreds of buffalo. That October, Mooar killed a rare albino buffalo.[14] Their outfit made a winter camp there and in the spring returned to Fort Phantom, which had become a shipping point for hides brought in by the hunters in the region. The next year, 1877, was the year of the great slaughter. McCombs and his crew of skinners and stakers took one thousand pounds of lead and five kegs of powder and slaughtered 9,700 buffalo in September of that year.

The buffalo were nearing extinction at this point. The introduction of the .50-caliber Sharps, or the Big Fifty as it was called, was so powerful that it enabled hunters to shoot farther with more deadly accuracy, but there was a movement to contain the slaughter even before this last fateful year.

In 1875, a bill was introduced in the Texas Legislature to protect the remaining animals but it was defeated. General Phillip Sheridan, one of General Sherman's advocates for extermination, came to Austin to speak against it. He argued that:

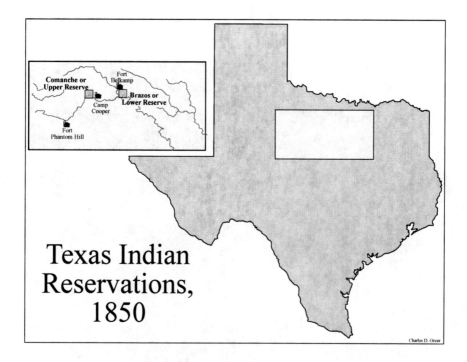

Texas Indian Reservations, 1850

Charles D. Grear

> These men [the buffalo hunters] have done in the last two years, and will do in the next year, more to settle the vexed Indian question than the entire regular Army has done in the last thirty years. They are destroying the Indian's commissary; and it is a well known fact that an army losing its base of supplies is placed at a great disadvantage. . . . Let them [the hunters] kill, skin and sell until the buffaloes are exterminated.[15]

The buffalo continued their decline until they were almost none to be found. Fortunately, there were those who recognized the buffalo would soon be extinct and moved to preserve them. As late as 1924, prominent rancher Charles Goodnight, gathered a few of the endangered animals and at the time of his death had a small herd of some two hundred head.[16]

By 1876, new counties had been formed out of the larger frontier lands. Taylor County, with Buffalo Gap as the county seat, was created in 1858 out of Bexar and Travis counties, and was officially organized with county officers in 1876 and the boundary lines were designated into their present-day position.[17]

The Texas & Pacific Railroad held a lot sale on March 15, 1881, and in 1882 the town of Abilene was incorporated. It soon became a major shipping point for hunters and immigrants in the developing area. With the Clear Fork of the Brazos

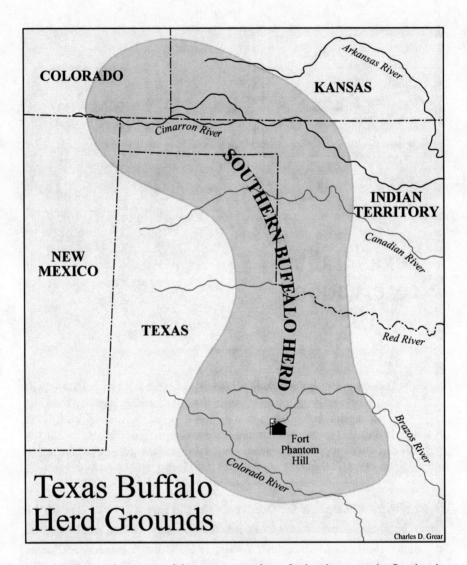

COLORADO

KANSAS

Arkansas River

Cimarron River

SOUTHERN BUFFALO HERD

INDIAN TERRITORY

Canadian River

NEW MEXICO

TEXAS

Red River

Fort Phantom Hill

Brazos River

Colorado River

Texas Buffalo Herd Grounds

Charles D. Grear

crossing the northern part of the area, a number of other large creeks flowing in the southern part of the county, and substantial grass for grazing, the development of the country around Fort Phantom was now inevitable, but with the new railroad through Abilene, Fort Phantom was destined to fade into history.

10
West Texas Begins to Develop

While Fort Griffin was engaged in dealing with the Indians, the stony monuments of old Fort Phantom became only a landmark for travelers. In 1858, Jones County, where the fort was located, was created by the Texas legislature out of Bexar and Bosque Counties and named for Anson Jones, the last president of the Republic of Texas. The remaining stonework of Fort Phantom Hill was the only evidence of habitation in the new county by anyone but transient Indians. It would be some fifteen years later before ranchers from the eastern part of the state moved their cattle into the county with the intent to settle there.

In 1873, brothers, John and Creed Roberts and J. G. and Mode Johnson settled in the southeastern part of the county, seeking land that was watered by some small streams and had ample grass. Their respective camps were five miles apart. Roberts related that: "We had an ideal cow country. Grass was abundant; the country was not overstocked as was the section east of us—in fact Johnson's and mine were all the cattle here for a while; the winters were mild and the country offered good protection."[1]

Because Indians were still a threat, the families moved their camps from time to time, hiding them in thickets or between close walls of draws or canyons. Their horses were always tethered close to camp and not allowed to wander.

At this time, buffalo were plentiful again but when the hunters from Fort Griffin came to gather their hides and tongues for sale in the east, cattlemen were spared the nuisance of the great herds that scored the land with deep trails and competed with their cattle for the grass. Roberts said: "I have seen the time when I could step out from our house or tent and shoot several early in the morning without moving from in front of the door."[2]

By 1879, Jones County was well populated with cattle and, to service the needs of the growing population, a small community developed around the old fort. Shipping the hides of the slain buffalo created the first civilian settlement, and a post office was established on July 1, 1879. The county held a population of some 546 individuals according to the 1880 census.[3]

There was excitement in the air for the Fort Phantom community when they heard news of the new Texas & Pacific Railway's plans to build their transcontinental route through west Texas. A small surge of land sales in anticipation of the railroad's construction collapsed when the decision was made to route it instead through Taylor County, where a land sale was held by the railroad and the city of Abilene was begun.

Although Jones County had been formed by the Texas legislature in 1858, it was not legally organized until 1881. The law creating the county permitted organization as soon as seventy-five "free, white, male inhabitants over the age of 21" petitioned to do so. In May 1881, the community of Fort Phantom was organized and became the temporary county seat of Jones County. By November of the same year, after three elections, the county seat moved to Anson and sealed the doom of the Fort Phantom settlement.[4] When the county seat moved, the population of Fort Phantom moved with it. Some went to the new county seat and others to the nearby town of Abilene.

In 1884, a visitor from Gatesville to the town of Fort Phantom noted that there were only three buildings standing. The Scott family was using one as a hotel and home. Another building served as a post office. The remaining structure was the old fort magazine.

By 1892 the town that had grown up around Fort Phantom had almost completely withered away. A letter written to the *San Antonio Express* that year reported that the little community consisted of "one hotel, one saloon, one general store, one blacksmith shop and 10,000 prairie dogs." By 1900, the little town no longer existed.[5] Most of the folks who knew the real history had moved on but, fortunately, the stone structures remained to create legends and stories about the mystery of the ruins.

Jones County, 1879

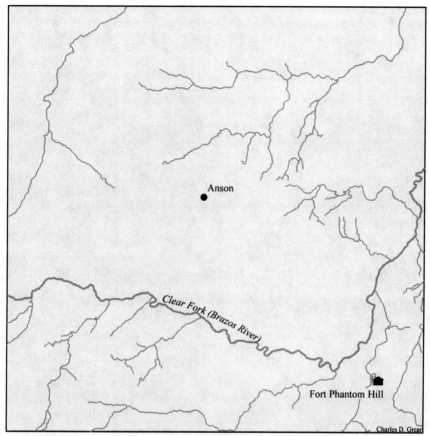

Several legends regarding the fort are recounted by historian H. Allen Anderson. One concerned a horse thief that was apprehended near Fort Phantom but maintained his innocence. He was given a "necktie" party but, before he died, he swore to return from the grave and deal his brand of justice to those who killed him. It was said that the man was later proved innocent and that those who had been involved in his summary execution all died mysterious deaths.

Another tale described the fort's being founded by Sam Houston who was said to be a frequent visitor. Some said the site of the old fort was once a gathering place for Indian outlaws and that it was a site for communing with the "Great Spirit." Others believed it once was the place where ritual sacrifices of animals took place and that the Aztecs from Mexico once came there.[6]

11

The End of the Frontier

The land on which the fort stood throughout its history was owned privately and was used in the later years as a pasture for cattle and storage for farm and ranch supplies by a succession of owners. In 1928, John Guitar purchased the land, but there was growing interest in the historic nature of the ruins.

One of the first persons to exhibit interest in the history of the fort was Carl Coke Rister, professor of history at Hardin-Simmons University in Abilene. Serving as the secretary of the West Texas Historical Association, headquartered at the university, he researched the history of the fort in War Department records in Washington and elsewhere, publishing numerous articles in a variety of publications. He believed the fort should be preserved and urged "patriotic citizens of this portion of the state" to purchase it for preservation.[1]

To a certain extent, he was successful in drawing attention to the old fort. During the Texas Centennial of 1936, a bronze marker was placed at the fort, but the owners at the time still had paramount agricultural interests. The land within the fort was farmed, and one of the buildings was used as an animal shelter. The early photographs of the fort were made during this time by a local photographer, Ray Rector, many of whose collected works are located at the University of Texas at Austin.

In 1969, John Guitar sold the Fort Phantom property to his grandson, Jim Alexander of Abilene. Albany historian and civic worker, Clifton Caldwell, a

Fort Phantom Hill (near Albany, Texas), established in 1851 to protect against Indians, ca. 1925. Courtesy of Ray Rector. University of Texas-Austin. Discrete Collection 140.1. 997:0051:0078.

Jim Alexander at Fort Phantom, 2012. Courtesy of Bill Wright, author.

member of the Texas Historical Survey Committee, focused interest on the ruins, and in 1970, it was officially recognized as a Texas historic site. In 1971 a state archaeology team under the direction of Curtis Tunnell, the State Archaeologist,

Fort Phantom Hill (near Albany, Texas), chimney. Courtesy of Ray Rector. University of Texas-Austin. Discrete Collection 140.1. 997:0051:0079.

surveyed the site of Fort Phantom making surface collections and photographing the extant structures.

The fort was truly valued as a historic resource when it was acquired by the Alexander family, who fortunately protected it from vandalism. The old military road that once ran through the fort now constitutes a portion of FM 600 that runs

Fort Phantom Hill (near Albany, Texas), chimney. Courtesy of Ray Rector. University of Texas-Austin. Discrete Collection 140.1. 997:0051:0082.

Fort Phantom Hill (near Albany, Texas. Courtesy of Ray Rector. University of Texas-Austin. Discrete Collection 140.1. 997:0051:0083.

from Abilene to Avoca, carrying considerable traffic and thus rendering the site vulnerable to predation. Before Alexander's ownership, even some of the building stone from the old fort was used in the construction of Abilene homes.

In 1997, the Alexander family contributed the land on which the fort stands to the Fort Phantom Foundation, establishing a legal entity that would operate and care for the site. Soon, the foundation commissioned a more detailed archaeological investigation of the site, and in 1998, archaeologists from Texas Tech University under the direction of archaeologist Dr. Grant Hill made a detailed analysis. Martha Doty Freeman prepared an extensive report on the fort's history and architecture. Steps were also taken to stabilize the crumbling stonework and ensure easier access for visitors.

From time to time, the Fort Phantom Foundation sponsors a historical celebration at the site. In 1972, to formally open the facilities to the public, the Fort Phantom Foundation sponsored a "Boots and Saddles" celebration attended by more than a thousand persons. Troopers from the First Calvary Horse Platoon from Fort Hood, dressed in uniforms appropriate to the nineteenth century, performed a riding and saber drill for the crowd. The president emeritus of Hardin-Simmons University, historian Rupert N. Richardson, spoke on the history of the fort.[2]

There continues to be historical enactments with history students from McMurry University in Abilene playing the roles of various soldiers who were once stationed at the fort.

Fort Phantom Hill (near Albany, Texas), Chimney, ca. 1925. Courtesy of Ray Rector. University of Texas-Austin. Discrete Collection 140.1. 997:0051:0084.

Fort Phantom Hill, powder magazine. Courtesy of Ray Rector. University of Texas-Austin. Discrete Collection 140.1. 997:0051:0087.

Fort Phantom Hill, refractory ruins, ca. 1927. Courtesy of Ray Rector. University of Texas-Austin. Discrete Collection 140.1. 997:0051:0088.

Fort Phantom Hill ruins, ca. 1927. Courtesy of Ray Rector. University of Texas-Austin. Discrete Collection 140.1. 997:0051:0089.

C. L. English and family at Fort Phantom Hill, near Albany, Texas. English had first newspaper. Courtesy of Ray Rector. University of Texas-Austin. Discrete Collection 140.1. 997:0051:0133.

* * *

Perhaps the most important event in the history of the West Texas frontier was not the decline of the buffalo or the defeat and pacification of the various Indian tribes. Rather, it was the extension of the Texas Pacific Railroad through the Fort Phantom country. Ironically, plans had been made by the owners of the Houston & Texas Central Railroad to extend their Austin branch north through Travis County

Historical Reenactment, 1972. Courtesy of Bill Wright, author.

Historical Reenactment, 1972. Courtesy of Bill Wright, author.

all the way to Fort Phantom Hill, where it was to be connected with the Texas Pacific railroad. Unfortunately, the Texas Pacific main route west later changed to pass through the future town of Abilene in Taylor County; had it not, the history of old Fort Phantom and the community that grew up around it would surely have been much different.

Historical Reenactment, 1972. Courtesy of Bill Wright, author.

Historical Reenactment, 1972. Courtesy of Bill Wright, author.

Steam transportation soon replaced horses and wagons, and commercial development supplanted the small trading posts that had furnished goods and services for those on the frontier. The age of trails that had formed the transportation system since the first immigrants arrived on foot many thousands of years gave way to steam and ribbons of steel.[3]

Historical Reenactment, 1972. Courtesy of Bill Wright, author.

Even though the old fort that was located in the wrong place, was staffed with foot soldiers instead of cavalry, and ultimately suffered the indignity of being burned, it still survives as a physical monument to those earlier days of conflict and turmoil. Along with the other frontier forts that helped make the West safe for settlers, Fort Phantom takes its place with others who helped "win" the West. Although troops there never engaged the enemy in any colorful skirmishes claiming many killed or captured, it fulfilled a psychological role. The fort's presence demonstrated to the Indians that the settlers planned to stay and that the United States would continue to take steps to ensure their safety.

It is interesting to speculate what might have been had General William Goldsmith Belknap not fallen ill. The general had a record of competence during his service in three wars, being twice wounded and three times brevetted for gallantry, distinguished conduct, and faithful service. During his meeting with General Persifor F. Smith, however, he was consumed with disease, possibly typhoid with its accompanying high fever and diarrhea. He was not at the peak of his vigor. Had he been well, it is possible to believe that his argument regarding the future site of Fort Phantom Hill could have carried the day. The fort would have then been located where there were ample building materials at hand and adequate water, even to this day. With these critical elements in place, it is conceivable that there would have been no necessity for the future Fort

Historical Reenactment, 1972. Courtesy of Bill Wright, author.

Chadbourne, and the post at General Belknap's location might have continued until the end of the Indian Wars.

If this had happened, the route of the Butterfield Overland mail would no doubt have been changed, and perhaps the location of the future county seat of

Jones County. Even the transcontinental railroad that once considered a route near Fort Phantom Hill would perhaps have changed. All of this is speculation, of course, but history often turns on the illness of a general.

Today, the lonely, empty chimneys beckon to tourists and kindles in some of them a desire to know their history and the history of their state. Perhaps sparking this historical curiosity, causing people to ask themselves "what if . . ?" will ultimately be Fort Phantom Hill's greatest contribution.

Partial List of Soldiers Stationed at Fort Phantom Hill

First US Infantry[1]

Company D

      Captain Seth Eastman, left company July 16, 1856

      Sergeant John Ford, joined February 20, 1857

      Corporal Samuel Gordon, joined February 21, 1857

      Private John Hart, joined February 23, 1857

      First Lieutenant Samuel B. Halabird, absent since date of transfer

      First Sergeant John Lynch, joined February 24, 1857

      Second Lieutenant Henry C. Woods since Jan. 15, 1857

Companies of the Fifth US Infantry[2,3]

Brevet Lieutenant Colonel John Joseph Abercrombie succeeded by Lieutenant Colonel Carlos A. Waite

Company B (47 men)

      Captain J. C. Robinson

      Second Lieutenant William H. Lewis

Company C (37 men)

      Captain S. H. Fowler

      Lieutenant B. Wingate

Alexander Giddis
Z. M. Giddis
Travis Gray
Francis Guy
Luke Hermall

Company E (48 men)
Second Lieutenant J. H. McArthur
First Lieutenant W. W. Burns

Company G (46 men)
Lieutenant F. T. Dint
August Glauty

Company K (41 men)
Captain N. B. Rossell
First Lieutenant C. W. Lear
Lieutenant D. C. Stith.

Company Unknown

Robert Hammell	Daniel Smith Lee
Thomas Hern	Edward M. Lee
George T. Hofman	Elias Less
William Gates Le Duc	Elmo Mullins Carl Lee
Augustus Canfield Ledyard	Fitzhugh Lee
Henry Brockholst Ledyard	Fitzhugh Lee, Jr.
Albert Lindley Lee	Francis Lee
Alexander Nisbet Lee	George W. Thomas
Archibald Lee	Hanson A. Thomas
Arthur Tracy Lee [PA]	Henry Goddard Thomas
Arthur Tracy Lee [MA]	Horace Holmes Thomas
Benjamin F. Lee	James Thomas
Bradley David Lee	James Augustus Thomas
Charles Lee	Jeremiah Thomas
Charles Carroll Lee	Jerome Beers Thomas
Charles Cochrane Lee	John Thomas
Charles W. Lee	John A. Thomas
Daniel Mortimer Lee	John Addison Thomas

John M. Thomas

John Robert Thomas, Jr.

John W. Thomas

Lorenzo Thomas

Lorenzo Thomas, Jr.

Martin Thomas

Minor T. Thomas

Philip Kearney Thomas

Pierce Thomas

Richard Morgan Thomas

Letters from Brevet Major General Persifor F. Smith and Brevet Lieutenant Colonel J. J. Abercrombie

Headquarters 8th Military Department
Camp Belknap, Red Fork of Brazos River, Texas
November 3, 1851
Order No. 91

Bt. Brig General Belknap, Lt. Col. 5th Inf, having selected the present site on the Red Fork of the Brazos; and at the intimation of myself, another on the Clear Fork of the same river at or in the immediate vicinity of a point known as Phantom Hill they are hereby established as military forts.

The buildings will be created according to the plans furnished—every attention being paid to economy. Each of the posts will be garrisoned by a wing of the 5th Infty and the left wing of that regiment will immediately be put in motion under the direction of Bvt. Lt Colonel Abercrombie to occupy the site selected on the Clear Fork.

The Regimental Headquarters will be established with the right wing.

Signed. Persifor F Smith

Bt Major General

Comd of 8th Mil Dept.

Asst. Adj. Genls' Office, 8th Dept

San Antonio, November 19, 1851 Official:

Signed: Geo. Deas

Asst Adj. Gen'l[1]

Evidently, Abercrombie was given additional assignments in advance of the written orders. A letter to the general dated October 26, 1851, requested items for the post that was to be established on the Concho River.

To Genl R. Jones

Adjt Genl. Of Army

Washington, D.C.

Brazos River, Texas

October 26, 1851

Genl,

I have the honor to request that the Post at Concho River about to be established be furnished with the following blanks from Company B.

Blank Post Returns

Discharges

Surgeons' certificate of disability

Ordinary and Pension

+model Post returns

Please direct them via San Antonio, Texas

Very Respectively

Your Obn't Servt.

J. J. Abercrombie

Bt. Lt. Col USA

Maj 5th Inf.[2]

Letter to Brevet Major General Persifor F. Smith

November 14, 1853

Letter to Bvt. Major General P. F. Smith, Army Department of Texas, Corpus Christi, Texas, from S. Cooper, Adj. Genrl. [On outside of original letter: Records of the Headquarters of the U.S. Army, Letters Received, #A 184 (1853)]

General,

Your communication of September 4,—in relation to the removal and control of the Indians in Texas, has been referred to this office by the Secretary of War, by whom I am instructed to say, in reply, that your views in relation thereto meet the approval of the Department.

Your recommendation that a new post be established on the Rio Grande, at or near Presidio Del Norte, is also approved; but before any final orders are given, it is considered important that the site should be selected by a competent officer, and that the best information should be obtained of the character of the country, and the facilities it may afford in building materials and other resources, as well as the positive certainty of the navigability of the Rio Grande for the transportation of supplies. These are deemed essential preliminaries. Taking into consideration the objects for which this post is designated, it should be garrisoned by not less than six companies.

Your recommendations for withdrawing the Infantry from the posts on the upper line, and for abandoning the post at Phantom Hill, is approved. And will be carried into execution. The Secretary also directs the Fort Territt and Mason be abandoned; (he cannot see the necessity of retaining the latter, merely as a depot) and that only Fort Belknap, Chadbourne, and McKavitt, be retained on that line, each to be garrisoned by two companies of Dragoons.

In view also of the heavy expense that will attend the establishment of the new post at Fort Ewell, and as the same results may be attained by a different disposition of the mounted Rifleman, the Secretary of War is of the opinion that this post should not be established and that the companies of that Regiment should be distributed along the Rio Grande from Ringgold Barracks to Eagle Pass and including Fort Clarke.

The necessary estimates for Banache will be made here to conform to suggestions.

The Secretary of War desires that in posting the troops in your Department, reference be had to keeping the companies of the same Regiments as much as possible in the same geographical neighborhoods; and as the post about to be established at Pass Del Norte will, after a short time, be again under your orders, that fact should be considered in designation the Infantry portion of the garrison for the post proposed to be established at the Presidio Del Norte, and the Infantry companies withdrawn from the upper line.

The companies of the 7th Infantry will be withdrawn from your Department as soon as the circumstances of the service will permit and the companies of the Rifle Regiment lately on the plains will immediately be ordered to Texas if they should not be required in the Cherokee county this winter.

The importance of finding comfortable quarters for the troops on the frontier is fully appreciated by the Secretary of War.

And it is his intention that this shall be done so far as the means may be provided by Congress. To accomplish this with the least expense to the government, it is necessary that the troops should be as much concentrated as possible; and this course will no doubt add to their efficiency and usefulness.

Until the contemplated arrangements with regard to the Indians of Texas have been carried out, the troops at Fort Belknap (now within the limits of the Department of the West) will be subject to your orders.[1]

Charles Goodnight Correspondence[1]

immons

C.Goodnight.

I. When and where were you born ? Macouphin Co.Ill.
March,5,1836

II. Where and under whom did you serve during the civil war ? Frontier West Texas. Undre Captain Jack Cureton of the Texas Rangers

III. Where did you settle when you came to west Texas ?

    A. Present town---Near Cameron Milam County--
    B. Direction from--Xx East of Cameron---------
    C. Miles from------Ten Miles-------------

IV. When did you come to west Texas ? Palo Pinto Co.1857.

V. How long did you market at Trinidad ? Two years---
---------- Ft. Dodge (Dodge City) Three years
Withita Falls Two yrs-, Henerelta Never---
Wichita Falls

VI. When did you open the trail to xxxxxxxxx ? 1883 or 84

VII. How many men usually went on a drive to market ? 12 to 14

-------- How long did it take to drive a herd of cattle
Dodge City
to xxxxxxxx ? 22 days

VIII. What trouble did you have with the Indians ? None

With thieves ? Country was full of thieves and desperadoes

With Stampedes ? Nothing unusual in this territory.

    IX. Did the cattle thrive on these drives ? Yes when
    prperly handled
    X. What prices were paid for cattle ? two to three cents

    XI. What were the wages of the cowboys ? $25.00 to 50.00

    XII. What about the closing of free range ?----

When ? In the 80s   Any fence cutting ? Very little

Any indictments ? None------   Who was responsible for the

cutting ? Largely cattlemen

    XIII. About ranch life. --------
Home life of women. -----

immons

Education.**First school at old Clarendon about 1879 financed
by the cattlemen's association**

Religious........**Christian colony settled at Old Clarendon about
1878. Had services at J.A. Ranch from twice a month from
about 1878**

XIV. How many soldiers were stationed at Ft.Eliot? **Three or four
companies**

XV. What tribe of Indians were nearest ? **Comanches and Kiowas**

When did you make the treaty with Quanah Parker ? **Spring of
1878**

XVI. When did you and John Adair began to capture buffaloe ?
**Adair had nothing to do with buffalo. Calves were captured
in 1878**

What were the size of the herds ? **They were extremely
scarce in 1878**

Where did they range ? **From the Colorado River North to
the Black Hills of Dakota.**

Do you know the price paid for hides ? **.50 to $1.00**

If so what ?---

XVII. When did you cross the cow and Buffaloe? **In the early
eighties**

XVIII. When did you cross the sheep and hog ? **About 1920**

That name did you give it ? **Nevre named it**

XIX. When did you give the Baptist the college at Goodnight ?-
About 1909 . When did it burn **1919 after turned over to
Buckner Orphans Home**

When used as an Orphans Home **1918 to 1920** When returned to you?
1920

XX. When was the cattle association organised in that section?
About 1878

XXI. How many Buffaloe are on the ranch now ? **200** How
many cattle ? **40 or 50** How many sheep-Hogs **None** How many
hogs ?-----

Notes

Introduction

1. Mary Hampton Clack, *Early Days in West Texas* (1932), 97. Reprinted in Duff, Katherine, *Pioneer Days . . . Two Views* (Abilene, Texas: Zachry Associates, Inc., 1979), 119.
2. Clack, *Early Days in West Texas*, 97.
3. Military records and archaeological investigations do not suggest that such embankments ever existed at the fort or others constructed on the Texas frontier.
4. Clack, *Early Days in West Texas*, 95.

Chapter 1

1. John Taylor Hughes, *Doniphan's Expedition* (Chicago: Rio Grande Press, 1962), 21–36.
2. Mike Kingston, "A Brief Sketch of Texas History," *The Texas Almanac 2006–2007*, ed. Elizabeth Cruce Alvarez (Dallas: *The Dallas Morning News*, 2006), 50, 56.
3. Donald S. Frazier, *Blood and Treasure* (College Station: Texas A&M Press, 1995).
4. Robert P. Wetteman, Jr., "Siege of Fort Texas," *The United States and Mexico at War: Nineteenth-Century Expansionism and Conflict*, edited by Donald S. Frazier. (New York: Simon and Schuster, 1998), 162. After the attack, Fort Texas was renamed Fort Brown in honor of Major Jacob Brown who was killed during the engagement.

Chapter 2

1. A. B. Bender, "The Texas Frontier, 1848–1860," *Southwestern Historical Quarterly* 38, No. 2 (October 1934), 135.
2. A. B. Bender, "Opening Routes Across West Texas, 1848–1850," *Southwestern Historical Quarterly* 37, No.2 (October 1933), 116.
3. Rupert N. Richardson, *The Comanche Barrier to South Plains Settlement* (Abilene, Texas: Hardin-Simmons University, 1991), 44.

4. Bryan Woolley, *Texas Almanac 2004–2005* (Dallas: *The Dallas Morning News*, 2004), 16.

5. Robert M. Utley, *The Indian Frontier 1846–1890*, Rev. Ed. (Albuquerque: University of New Mexico Press, 2003), 2; H. Allen Anderson, "Fort Phantom Hill: Outpost on the Clear Fork of the Brazos," *The Museum Journal of Texas Tech University XVI* (1976), 14.

6. "Marcy, Randolph Barnes (1812–1887)," *Encyclopedia of Oklahoma History and Culture*, accessed September 19, 2012, at http://digital.library.okstate.edu /encyclopedia/entries/M/MA021.html.

7. Utley, *The Indian Frontier*, 2.

8. Bender, "Opening Routes Across West Texas 1848–1850," 116.

9. Roy L. Swift "Chihuahua Expedition," *New Handbook of Texas* (Austin: Texas State Historical Association, 2006), 76–77.

10. Ben G. O'Neal. "The Beginnings of Fort Belknap," *Southwestern Historical Quarterly* vol. 61, no. 4 (April 1958), 509.

11. Walter Prescott Webb, *The Texas Rangers: A Century of Frontier Defense*, 2nd ed. (Austin: University of Texas Press, 1965), 127.

12. Edward S. Wallace, "General William Jenkins Worth and Texas," *Southwestern Historical Quarterly* vol. 54, no. 2 (October 1950), 167.

13. Daniel E. Fox, *Traces of Texas History: Archaeological Evidence of the Past 450 Years* (San Antonio: Corona Publishing Co., 1983), 260.

14. Malcolm D. McLean, "Robertson, Elijah Sterling Clack," *The New Handbook of Texas*, vol.5, edited by Ron Tyler. (Austin: Texas State Historical Association, 1996), 615–616.

15. Anderson, "Outpost on the Clear Fork of the Brazos," 5.

16. Allen G. Hatley, *Bringing the Law to Texas* (LaGrange, Texas: Centex Press, 2002), 27.

Chapter 3

1. Ed Bearss and Arrell M. Gibson, *Fort Smith: Little Gibraltar on the Arkansas* (Norman: University of Oklahoma Press, 1967), 145–167.

2. Bearss and Gibson, *Fort Smith*, 191.

3. Donald D. Mawson, "The Federal Military Defense of the Northwest Texas Frontier," 1846–1861, Master's Thesis (Hardin-Simmons University, Abilene, Texas, 1971), 51.

4. Martha Doty Freeman, *A History of Fort Phantom Hill: The Post on the Clear Fork of the Brazos River, Jones County, Texas* (Abilene: The Fort Phantom Foundation, 1999), 8–9.

5. Rupert N. Richardson, ed., "Documents Relating to West Texas and Its Indian Tribes," *West Texas Historical Association Yearbook* (1925), 34.

6. Anderson, "Outpost on the Clear Fork of the Brazos," 12.

7. Col. M. L. Crimmins, "The First Line of Army Posts Established in West Texas in 1849," *West Texas Historical Association Year Book* XIX (October 1943), 121–126.

8. W. C. Holden, "Frontier Defense, 1846–1860," *West Texas Historical Association Year Book* (June 1930), 49.

9. A. B. Bender, "The Texas Frontier, 1848–1860 Part II," *Southwestern Historical Quarterly* vol. 38, no.2 (October 1934), 135–148.
10. Anderson, "Outpost on the Clear Fork of the Brazos," 8.
11. Linda S. Hudson, *Mistress of Manifest Destiny: A Biography of Jane McManus Storm Cazneau 1807–1878* (Austin: Texas State Historical Association, 2001), 135.
12. Hudson, *Mistress of Manifest Destiny*, 135.
13. M. L. Crimmins, "Notes and Documents: W. G. Freeman's Report on the Eighth Military Department (Continued)," *Southwestern Historical Quarterly* (October 1949), 204–208.
14. Charles G. Downing, and Roy L. Swift, "Howard, Richard Austin," *The New Handbook of Texas*, Vol.3 (Austin: Texas State Historical Association, 1996), 744–745.
15. Belknap had steadfastly refused to contribute men from his understaffed unit for the building of Fort Smith, even after repeated orders to do so. George H. Shirk, "Mail Call at Fort Washita," *The Chronicles of Oklahoma* XXXIII, Spring (1955), 14–35.
16. Shirk, "Mail Call at Fort Washita," 17–18.
17. Freeman, *A History of Fort Phantom Hill*, 17.
18. R. B. Marcy, "Report of Captain R. B. Marcy, of The Fifth Infantry, United States Army, On His Exploration of Indian Territory and Northwest Texas," *West Texas Historical Association Year Book* XIV (1938), 126–127.

Chapter 4

1. Fifty years later, in his memoir, a valuable description of life on the frontier, Jeff Maltby wrote his firsthand account of the expedition to establish these frontier forts, specifically, Fort Phantom Hill, near the present city of Abilene, Texas. The two versions of the actual founding of the fort—the official records of the War Department and the correspondence between the officers involved and a second account written by Maltby—are similar but there are significant differences. Historian Rupert Richardson, writing the foreword in Maltby's book, *Captain Jeff: Frontier Life in Texas with the Texas Rangers*, observed that perhaps the years separating the event had caused Maltby to forget some of the details. He was mistaken about the leader of the expedition, the date, and other smaller facts according to Richardson, but he believed the details about the trip itself were generally accurate.
2. Preston was a frontier town located on the Washita Bend of the Red River. Founded by Holland Coffee, Preston was a key location that began as a trading post in 1837. It became a US Army depot in 1851 to supply the Fifth Infantry under the command of Lt. Thomas C. English and later, Bvt. Maj. W. F. Wood.
3. Rupert N Richardson, *The Frontier of Northwest Texas: Frontier Military Series V* (Cleveland: Arthur H. Clark Company, 1963), 63.
4. Anderson, "Outpost on the Clear Fork of the Brazos," 16.
5. O'Neal, "The Beginnings of Fort Belknap," 516.
6. Shirk, "Mail Call at Fort Washita," 23.
7. Shirk, "Mail Call at Fort Washita," 24.
8. Freeman, *A History of Fort Phantom Hill*, 62.

9. Michael Baldridge, *A Reminiscence of the Parker H. French Expedition through Texas & Mexico to California in the Spring of 1850* (Los Angeles: John B. Goodman III, 1959), 12.

10. William J. Maltby, *Captain Jeff or Frontier Life in Texas with the Texas Rangers* (Waco, Texas: Texian Press, 1967), 129.

11. Maltby, *Captain Jeff*, 130.

12. Maltby, *Captain Jeff*, 132.

13. Maltby, *Captain Jeff*, 132.

14. Anderson, "Outpost on the Clear Fork of the Brazos," 17.

15. Anderson, "Outpost on the Clear Fork of the Brazos," 17.

16. Anderson, "Outpost on the Clear Fork of the Brazos," 17.

17. National Archives and Records Service. General Service Administration. Microcopy, no.617, roll 141. The muleskinner, W. J. Maltby also assisted. Frances Mayhugh Holden, *Lambshead Before Interwoven: A Texas Range Chronicle 1848–1878* (College Station: Texas A&M University Press, 1982), 40.

18. Ralph A. Smith, "Old West Texas Limekilns Are Mostly Mysteries, Memories, and Material Remains," *West Texas Historical Association Year Book* LII (1976), 30.

19. Anderson, "Outpost on the Clear Fork of the Brazos," 22.

20. Shirk, "Mail Call at Fort Washita," 23.

21. Anderson, "Outpost on the Clear Fork of the Brazos," 21.

22. Emma Johnson Elkins, "Old Fort Phantom and Its Tragedies," *Hunter's Magazine* (1911), 21.

23. Freeman, *A History of Fort Phantom Hill*, 62.

24. Anderson, "Outpost on the Clear Fork of the Brazos," 19.

25. Holden, *Lambshead Before Interwoven*, 12.

26. Freeman, *A History of Fort Phantom Hill*, 19.

27. M. L. Crimmins, (Ed.)., "W. G. Freeman's Report on the Eighth Military Department," *Southwestern Historical Quarterly* 53 (April. 1950), 448

28. Elkins, "Old Fort Phantom and Its Tragedies," 21.

29. M. L. Crimmins, ed., "Notes and Documents: W. G. Freeman's Report on the Eighth Military Department [Concluded]," *Southwestern Historical Quarterly* LIV, no. 2 (October 1950), 213.

30. M. L. Crimmins Papers, Surgeon Conally Report on Texas Forts, 1854, Center for American History, University of Texas, Austin. Hereafter cited as Crimmins Papers.

31. Crimmins Papers, "Surgeon Conally Report."

32. Elkins, "Old Fort Phantom and Its Tragedies," 21.

33. Carl Coke Rister, "The Border Post of Phantom Hill," *West Texas Historical Association Year Book XIV* (1938): 9.

Chapter 5

1. Anderson, "Outpost on the Clear Fork of the Brazos," 17.

2. Freeman, *A History of Fort Phantom Hill*, 74.

3. Anderson, "Outpost on the Clear Fork of the Brazos," 35.

4. Anderson, "Outpost on the Clear Fork of the Brazos," 33.

5. James O. Breeden, "Health of Early Texas: The Military Frontier," *Southwestern Historical Quarterly* LXXX, no. 4 (April 1977), 393.
6. Anderson, "Outpost on the Clear Fork of the Brazos," 20.
7. Crimmins, "Notes and Documents," 169.
8. E. L. Deaton, *Indian Fights on the Texas Frontier* (Fort Worth: Pioneer Publishing Company/The Bunker Press, 1927), 4.
9. First Lieutenant William W. Burns, Phantom Hill, Texas, to Com. Gen. Subsistence Bvt. Maj. Gen. Gov. Gibbons, Washington, September 3, 1853. National Archives Record Group No. 92, Records of the Quartermaster General's Office Consolidated Correspondence File.
10. W. G. Freeman, "Report of Inspection of 8th Military Department Made by Bvt. Lt. Col. W. G. Freeman, Asst. Adjt. Gen Pursuant to Instructions from Head Quarters of Army," April 22 1853, Crimmins Papers.
11. Freeman, "Report of Inspection," Crimmins Papers.
12. Linda S. Hudson, *Mistress of Manifest Destiny: A Biography of Jane McManus Storm Cazneau 1807–1878* (Austin: Texas State Historical Association: 2001): 130.
13. Crimmins, "W. G. Freeman's Report on the Eighth Military Department," 451.
14. Freeman, "Report of Inspection," Crimmins Papers.
15. Sandra L. Myres, "Fort Graham: Listening Post on the Texas Frontier," *West Texas Historical Association Yearbook LIX* (1983), 44.
16. Elkins, "Old Fort Phantom and Its Tragedies."
17. Jodyne Lynn Dickson and Thomas F. Schilz. *Buffalo Hump and the Penateka Comanches* (El Paso: Western Press, 1989), 37.
18. Noah Smithwick, *The Evolution of a State or Recollections of Old Texas Days*, edited by Alwyn Barr. (Austin: W. Thomas Taylor, 1995), 188.
19. Letter found in Appendix C.
20. Anderson, "Outpost on the Clear Fork of the Brazos," 42.
21. Anderson, "Outpost on the Clear Fork of the Brazos,"43.

Chapter 6

1. Anderson, "Fort Phantom Hill," 49.
2. Col. M. L. Crimmins. "The First Line of Army Posts Established in West Texas in 1849" *West Texas Historical Association Year Book* XIX (October 1943).
3. Anderson, "Fort Phantom Hill," 57.
4. Douglas Southall Freeman. *R. E. Lee* Vol. 1. (New York: Charles Scribner's Sons, 1936), 365.
5. Anderson, "Fort Phantom Hill," 50.
6. Joann Mazzio, "The Butterfield Overland Mail." *New Mexico Travel* (April 9, 2003), 1.
7. A. C. Greene. *900 Miles on the Butterfield Trail.* (Denton: University of North Texas Press, 1994), 35.
8. See, Celerity Wagon http://www.southernnewmexico.com/AuthorBios/BillKelly.html.
9. Glen Sample Ely. "Bedlam at Belknap: Frontier Lawlessness on the Butterfield Overland Mail Road in Texas, 1858–1861." *West Texas Historical Association Yearbook* LXXXII (2006): 81–101. The first comprehensive research done on the

route of the Southern Butterfield Overland Mail was done by a husband and wife team from El Paso, Roscoe and Margaret Conkling. Their work has been refined by the exhaustive research and field work of Glen Sample Ely in his master's thesis for Texas Christian University titled: "Riding the Western Frontier." A. C. Greene's location of the station was in error.

10. Mazzio, "The Butterfield Overland Mail," 89.
11. Greene, *900 Miles on the Butterfield Trail*, 35–36.
12. Greene, *900 Miles on the Butterfield Trail*, 48.
13. Greene, *900 Miles on the Butterfield Trail*, 49.
14. Greene, *900 Miles on the Butterfield Trail*, 49.
15. Walter B. Lang. *The First Overland Mail: Butterfield Trail, St. Louis to San Francisco 1858–1861* (New York: Roycrofters, 1940), 59.
16. H. Allen Anderson. "Mountain Pass: A Texas Frontier Landmark," *West Texas Historical Association Yearbook LIII* (1977), 58–67. Because Abercrombie was the first in the area to record landmarks, the pass is often referred to with his name. Later it is described as "Mountain Pass," Anderson, "Mountain Pass," 57–58.
17. Lang, *The First Overland Mail*, 59.
18. Lang, *The First Overland Mail*, 59.
19. W. L. Ormsby, *The Butterfield Overland Mail*, edited by L. H. Wright and J. M. Bynum. (San Marino, CA, 1954).
20. Glen Sample Ely, "Riding the Western Frontier: Antebellum Encounters Aboard the Butterfield Overland Mail." Fort Worth. Master's Thesis (Fort Worth: Texas Christian University, 2005), 177.
21. Travis Taylor, "Garrison Life at Fort Chadbourne, 1852–1861," *West Texas Historical Association Yearbook* vol. 87, no. 23 (2011), 27.
22. J. W. Williams. "The Butterfield Overland Mail Road Across Texas," *Southwestern Historical Quarterly* LXI (1957–1958), 8.

Chapter 7

1. T. R. Fehrenbach, *Lone Star* (Washington, D.C.: American Legacy Press, 1983), 326.
2. David Paul Smith, *Frontier Defense in the Civil War: Texas Rangers and Rebels* (College Station: Texas A&M University Press, 1992), 4.
3. According to David Paul Smith, there was no organized group officially known as "Texas Rangers" either before or after the war, until 1935 when they became part of the Texas Department of Public Safety.
4. Charles G. Davis, "Camp Cooper," *Handbook of Texas Online*, accessed October 18, 2012, ahttp://www.tshaonline.org/handbook/online/articles/qbc09.
5. Samuel P. Newcomb, *The Diary of Samuel P. Newcomb: January 1, 1865 to December 21, 1865* (Abilene: Private printing, 1964).
6. Ernest Wallace, "Mackenzie, Ranald Slidell," *Handbook of Texas Online*, accessed October 18, 2012 at http://www.tshaonline.org/handbook/online/articles/fma07.

Chapter 8

1. J. Evetts Haley, *Charles Goodnight: Cowman and Plainsman* (Norman: University of Oklahoma Press, 1949), 28–30.
2. Haley, *Charles Goodnight*, 186.
3. Anderson, "Fort Phantom Hill," 1113–1114. Vernon Lynch, "Fort Griffin (Shackleford County)," *The Handbook of Texas* Vol. II (Austin: Texas State Historical Association, 1996), 1102.
4. William H. Leckie, *The Buffalo Soldiers: A Narrative of the Negro Calvary in the West* (Norman: University of Oklahoma Press, 1967), 82–90.
5. Leckie, *The Buffalo Soliders*, 82–83.
6. Leckie, *The Buffalo Soliders*, 89–90.
7. Freeman, *A History of Fort Phantom Hill*, 94, 95.
8. Freeman, *A History of Fort Phantom Hill*, 94.
9. Freeman, *A History of Fort Phantom Hill*, 93.
10. Anderson, "Fort Phantom Hill," 63.
11. Freeman, *A History of Fort Phantom Hill*, 97.
12. Joe S. McCombs, "On the Cattle Trail, and Buffalo Range, Joe S. McCombs," *West Texas Historical Association Year Book* (1935), 93.
13. McCombs, "On the Cattle Trail," 94.
14. McCombs, "On the Cattle Trail," 95.
15. The "buffalo soldiers" stationed there were black troops that allegedly were given the nickname by the Indians because their black curly hair was reminiscent of the thick, shaggy, mane of the famous plains animal.
16. Leckie, *The Buffalo Soldiers*, 71.
17. Leckie, *The Buffalo Soldiers*, 73.

Chapter 9

1. Wayne Gard, "The Mooar Brothers, Buffalo Hunters," *Southwest Historical Quarterly* LXIII, no.1 (July 1959), 31–32.
2. Thomas J. DiLorenzo, "How Lincoln's Army 'Liberated' the Indians," accessed May 6, 2013, at http://lewrockwell.com/dilorenzo/dilorenzo40.html.
3. DiLorenzo, "How Lincoln's Army 'Liberated' the Indians."
4. S. C. Gwynne, *Empire of the Summer Moon: Quanah Parker and the Rise and Fall of the Comanches, the Most Powerful Indian Tribe in American History* (New York: Scribner, 2010), 5.
5. Virginia H. Taylor Houston, "Surveying in Texas," *Southwestern Historical Quarterly* 65 (October 1961), 229.
6. Ty Cashion, *A Texas Frontier: The Clear Fork Country and Fort Griffin, 1849–1887* (Norman: University of Oklahoma Press, 1996), 170.
7. Charles Robinson III, *The Frontier World of Fort Griffin: The Life and Death of a Western Town, Western Lands and Water Series* vol. XVII (Spokane, Washington: Arthur H. Clark Company, 1992), 56.
8. Robinson III, *The Frontier World of Fort Griffin*, 56.

9. "Council Deliberates Fates of Santanta & Big Tree," *The Springfield Republican*, August 6, 1873, accessed September 26, 2012, at http://theoldentimes.com /santantabigtree.html.

10. "Texas Beyond History," accessed May 6, 2013, at http://www.texasbeyondhistory .net/redriver/index.html

11. Gard, "The Mooar Brothers, Buffalo Hunters," 31–45.

12. Allen G. Hatley. *Bringing the Law to Texas: Crime and Violence in Nineteenth Century Texas* (LaGrange, Texas: Centex Press, 2002).

13. Gard, "The Mooar Brothers, Buffalo Hunters," 38.

14. Robinson III, *The Frontier World of Fort Griffin*, 56.

15. "Scotty Philip, the Man Who Saved the Buffalo," Philip Chamber of Commerce, accessed October 1, 2012, http://www.philipsouthdakota.com/other_7.html.

16. J. M. Sibley, Correspondence with Charles Goodnight, (1924), letter in Goodnight Archive, Hardin-Simmons University Richardson Library. See Letters in Appendix D.

17. L. L. Foster, *Forgotten Texas Census* (Austin: Texas State Historical Association, 2001), 210.

Chapter 10

1. Homer Hutto and Hooper Shelton, *Jones County, Texas: The First 100 Years* (Stamford, Texas: Shelton Press, 1978), 32.

2. Hutto and Shelton, *Jones County, Texas*, 33.

3. Hutto and Shelton, *Jones County, Texas*, 35.

4. Hutto and Shelton, *Jones County, Texas*, 35.

5. Anderson, "Outpost on the Clear Fork of the Brazos," 76.

6. Anderson, "Outpost on the Clear Fork of the Brazos," 78.

Chapter 11

1. Anderson, "Outpost on the Clear Fork of the Brazos," 82

2. B. P. Gallaway, "History in West Texas," *West Texas Historical Association Year Book* XLVIII, (1972), 165.

3. J. W. Williams, "Military Roads of the 1850's in Central West Texas," *West Texas Historical Association Year Book* XVIII October 1942), 77.

Appendix: Partial List of Soldiers Stationed at Fort Phantom Hill

1. Roll 1531, M617.

2. Anderson, "Outpost on the Clear Fork of the Brazos," 17.

3. "Report of Inspection of 8th Military Department Made by Brevet Lt. Col. W. G. Freeman, Asst. Adjunct. Gen Pursuant to Instructions from Head Quarters of Army." M. L. Crimmins Paper Collection, Center for American History, University of Texas, Austin, April 22, 1853.

Appendix: Letters from Brevet Major General Persifor F. Smith and Brevet Lieutenant Colonel J. J. Abercrombie

1. O'Neal "The Beginnings of Fort Belknap," 515

2. Brazos River, Texas, to General R. Jones, Washington, D.C., October 26, 1851. Letters Received by the Adjunct General's Office 1822–1860: M-567, Roll 441 1851, Record 0507.

Appendix: Letter to Brevet Major General Persifor F. Smith

1. Adjutant General S. Cooper, Washington, D.C., to Brevet Major General P. F. Smith, Corpus Christi, November 4, 1853, 1853: Box No. 1117, Entry 225, RG92. National Archives.

Appendix: Charles Goodnight Correspondence

1. Sibley. J. M.. (1924). Correspondence with Charles Goodnight. Letter in Goodnight Archive, Hardin-Simmons University Richardson Library.

Bibliography

Abercrombie, Brevet Lieutenant Colonel J. J., Brazos River, Texas, to General R. Jones, Washington, D.C., October 26, 1851. Letters Received by the Adjutant General's Office 1822–1860: M-567, Roll 441, Record 0507, National Archives.

Abercrombie, Brevet Lieutenant Colonel J. J., Phantom Hill, Texas, to General R. Jones, November 25, 1851. Roll 441, M-567. National Archives.

Abercrombie, Brevet Lieutenant Colonel J. J., Red Fork, Brazos River, Texas, to Major General R. Jones, Washington, D.C., November 3, 1851. Letters Received by the Adjutant General's Office 1822–1860. Roll 441, Record 0505. National Archives.

Abercrombie, Brevet Lieutenant Colonel J. J., Department of Texas Headquarters. August 16, 1852. Washington, D.C., RG393, Vol. 2, Entry 4776. National Archives.

African Americans in Texas: Historical and Cultural Legacies. Austin: Texas Historical Commission. Accessed September 19, 2012, at http://creativefolk.com/travel/pdf/tx.afrcn_amrcn.pdf.

Anderson, H. Allen. "Fort Phantom Hill." *New Handbook of Texas*, 2: 113–114. Austin: Texas State Historical Association, 1996.

Anderson, H. Allen. "Fort Phantom Hill: Outpost on the Clear Fork of the Brazos." *The Museum Journal of Texas Tech University* 16 (1976), 1–104.

Anderson, H. Allen. "Mountain Pass: A Texas Frontier Landmark." *West Texas Historical Association Year Book* 53 (1977), 58–67.

Arbuckle, Brevet Brigadier General Matthew, Ft. Smith, Arkansas, to Brevet Lieutenant Colonel W. W. J. Bliss, New Orleans, Louisiana, May 18, 1851. Letters Received, 1852 [A-H], Box No. 5, Entry 5572, Part I, RG393. National Archives.

Arnold, James R. *Jeff Davis's Own*. Edison, NJ: Castle Books, 2007.

Bainbridge, Major and Brevet Lieutenant Colonel H., Fort Gibson, Cherokee Nation, to Western Division Brevet Lieutenant Colonel W. W. J. Bliss, June 20, 1851. Letters Received, 1851 [A-H], Box No. 5, Entry 5572, Part I, RG393. National Archives.

BIBLIOGRAPHY

Baldridge, Michael. *A Reminiscence of the Parker H. French Expedition through Texas and Mexico to California in the Spring of 1850.* Los Angeles: John B. Goodman III, 1959.

Barrett, Arrie. "Federal Military Outposts in Texas, 1846–1861." Ph. D. diss., University of Texas, 1927.

Barry, James Buckner. Papers, Box 2B44, Briscoe Center for American History, University of Texas, Austin.

Bartlett, John H., Washington, D.C., to Mr. Hybernia Grace, Anson, TX, June 22, 1928. Jones County, Texas, Collection, 1881–1961. Southwest Collection, Texas Tech University, Lubbock, Texas.

Bearss, Ed, and Arrell M. Gibson. *Fort Smith: Little Gibraltar on the Arkansas, Fort Phantom.* Norman: University of Oklahoma Press, 1967.

Bell, Hoffman and Klein. *Master Development Plan, Fort Phantom Hill, Jones County, Texas. Part One-Restoration/Stabilization.* Austin: Authors, 1977.

Bell, Walter F. "Civil War Texas: A Review of the Historical Literature." *Southwestern Historical Quarterly* vol. 109, no. 2 (October 2005), 205–232.

Bender, A. B. "Opening Routes across West Texas." *Southwestern Historical Quarterly* vol. 37, no. 2 (October 1933), 116–135.

Bender, A. B., "The Texas Frontier, 1848–1860 Part II." *Southwestern Historical Quarterly* vol. 38, no.2 (October 1934), 135–148.

Blair, Captain W. B., San Antonio, TX, to Major General George Gibson, Washington, D.C., October 19, 1852. In Box 342, Entry 225, RG92. National Archives.

Blair, W. B. *Report of an Inspection of the Subsistence Department in the 8th Military Department.* Corpus Christi, TX, July 17 1853. Box No. 1116, Entry 225, RG92. National Archives.

Boggess, H. H., Phantom Hill, Texas to Captain Barry, Camp Cooper, Texas, July 23, 1861. James Buckner Barry Papers, Briscoe Center for American History, University of Texas, Austin.

Braly, Earl Burk. "Fort Belknap of the Texas Frontier." *West Texas Historical Association Year Book* 30 (1954), 83–114.

Breeden, James O. "Health of Early Texas: The Military Frontier." *Southwestern Historical Quarterly* vol. 80 no. 4 (April 1977), 357–398.

Bristow, Michael. "Fort Phantom Hill". Typescript dated 1985 in the files of James Alexander, Abilene, Texas.

Bryan, Erin. "Diary of Erin Bryan, 1853." Ms. in Briscoe Center for American History, University of Texas, Austin.

Burns, Lieutenant William W., Post on Clear Fork Brazos River, to Major General Thomas S. Jesup, Washington D.C., July 20, 1853. Box 342, Entry 225, RG92. National Archives.

Calhoun, Captain P., Fort Chadbourne, Texas, to Department of Texas Headquarters, January 17, 1855. Volume 2, Entry 4776, RG393. National Archives.

Calvert, Robert A., Arnoldo DeLeon, and Gregg Cantrell. *The History of Texas.* Wheeling, IL: Harlan Davidson, Inc., 2007.

Carter, Robert G. *On the Border with Mackenzie, or Winning West Texas from the Comanches.* New York Antiquarian Press, Ltd., 1961.

Cashion, Ty. *A Texas Frontier: The Clear Fork Country and Fort Griffin, 1849–1887.* Norman: University of Oklahoma Press, 1996.

Chapman, Captain William, Post on the Clear Fork of the Brazos River, Texas, to Major General R. Jones, Washington, D.C. January 20, 1852. Roll 459, M-567. National Archives.

Chipman, Donald E. "Jose Mares." *New Handbook of Texas* 4: 503. Austin: Texas State Historical Association, 1996.

Clack, Mary Hampton. *Early Days in West Texas.* Abilene, TX: Zachry Associates, 1977 [Repr. 1932].

Clayton, Lawrence, and Joan Halford Farmer, ed. *Tracks Along the Clear Fork: Stories from Shackelford and Throckmorton Counties.* Abilene, TX: McWhiney Foundation Press, 2000.

Clayton, Lawrence. "The Saga of the Stone Ranch." *West Texas Historical Association Year Book* 65 (1989), 70–77.

Coleman County History Comm. *A History of Coleman County and Its People.* San Angelo, TX: Anchor Publishing Co., 1986.

Conally, Surgeon. "Report on Texas Forts," in Crimmins Papers. Briscoe Center for American History, University of Texas, Austin.

Conkling, Roscoe P., and Margaret B. *The Butterfield Overland Mail, 1857–1869.* Volume I. Glendale, CA: The Arthur H. Clark Company, 1947–1948.

Cook, John R. *The Border and the Buffalo: An Untold Story of the Southwest Plains.* Austin: State House Press, 1989.

Cooper, Adjutant General S., Washington, D.C., to Brevet Major General P. F. Smith, Corpus Christi, November 4, 1853. Box No. 1117, Entry 225, RG92. National Archives.

Cooper, Colonel S. Washington D.C., to Department of Texas Headquarters, November 4, 1853. Volume 2, Entry 4776, RG393. National Archives.

Crane, R. C., ed. "Report of Captain R. B. Marcy, of the Fifth Infantry, United States Army, on His Exploration of Indian Territory and Northwest Texas." *West Texas Historical Association Year Book* 14 (1938),116–136.

Crane, R. C. "Some Aspects of the History of West and Northwest Texas since 1845." *Southwestern Historical Quarterly* vol. 26, no. 1 (July 1922), 30–43.

Crimmins, M. L., ed. "Extract from the Diary of Charles A. Crosby." *West Texas Historical Association Year Book* 17 (1941), 100–107.

Crimmins, M. L., ed. "Notes and Documents: W. G. Freeman's Report on the Eighth Military Department [Concluded]." *Southwestern Historical Quarterly* vol. 54, no. 2 (October 1950), 204–216.

Crimmins, M. L., ed. "Notes and Documents: W. G. Freeman's Report on the Eighth Military Department (Continued)." *Southwestern Historical Quarterly* vol. 51, no. 2 (October 1947), 168–174.

Crimmins, M. L., ed. "Notes and Documents: W. G. Freeman's Report on the Eighth Military Department (Continued)." *Southwestern Historical Quarterly* vol. 51, no. 4, (April 1947–1948), 350–357.

Crimmins, M. L. ed. "Notes and Documents: W. G. Freeman's Report on the Eighth Military Department (Continued)." *Southwestern Historical Quarterly* vol. 52, no. 1 (July 1949), 71–77.

BIBLIOGRAPHY

Crimmins, M. L. ed. "Notes and Documents: W. G. Freeman's Report on the Eighth Military Department (Continued)." *Southwestern Historical Quarterly* vol. 52, no. 2 (October, 1949), 202–208.

Crimmins, M. L. ed. "Notes and Documents: W. G. Freeman's Report on the Eighth Military Department (Continued)." *Southwestern Historical Quarterly* vol. 53, no. 3 (January 1950), 308–319.

Crimmins, M. L. ed. "Notes and Documents: W. G. Freeman's Report on the Eighth Military Department (Continued)." *Southwestern Historical Quarterly* vol. 53, no. 4 (April 1950), 443–473.

Crimmins, M. L. ed. "Notes and Documents: W. G. Freeman's Report on the Eighth Military Department (Continued)." *Southwestern Historical Quarterly* vol. 54, no. 2 (October 1950), 204–218.

Crimmins, M. L. "The First Line of Army Posts Established in West Texas in 1849." *West Texas Historical Association Year Book* 19 (1943), 121–127.

Crisp, James E. "Calculated Victory: Sam Houston's Campaign to Rescue the Texas Revolution." *Proceedings: The Philosophical Society of Texas* 68 (December 2004), 29–37.

Crouch, Carrie J. *A History of Young County, Texas.* Austin: Texas State Historical Association, 1956.

Crouch, Carrie J. *Fort Belknap.* Graham, Texas: The Graham Leader, 1952.

Crouch, Carrie J. *Young County History and Biography.* Dallas: Dealey and Lowe, 1937.

Cutrer, Thomas W. "David Murphree." *The New Handbook of Texas.* Austin: Texas State Historical Association, 1996.

Dearen, Patrick. *Castle Gap and the Pecos Frontier.* Fort Worth: Texas Christian University Press, 1988.

Dearen, Patrick. *Crossing Rio Pecos.* Fort Worth: Texas Christian University Press, 1996.

Deaton, E. L. *Indian Fights on the Texas Frontier.* Fort Worth: Pioneer Publishing Company, 1927.

Dent, First Lieutenant F. T., New Post on Clear Fork of Brazos, to Brevet Major General George Gibson, Washington, D.C., April 8, 1852. Box 342, Entry 225, RG92. National Archives.

Dent, First Lieutenant F. T., New Post on Clear Fork of Brazos, to Brevet Major General George Gibson, Washington, D.C. Box 342, Entry 225, RG92. National Archives.

Dent, First Lieutenant F. T., New Post on Phantom Hill, Texas, to Major General Thomas S. Jesup, Washington, D.C., January 3, 1852. Box No. 1217, Entry 225, RG92. National Archives.

DeVoto, Bernard. *The Year of Decision: 1846.* Boston: Little, Brown and Company, 1943.

Dillard , Richard, Abilene, Texas, to Truett Latimer, Austin, Texas, May 12, 1975. Copy in files of Rick Weatherl, Abilene, Texas.

DiLorenzo, Thomas J. "How Lincoln's Army 'Liberated' the Indians." Accessed May 6, 2013, at http://lewrockwell.com/dilorenzo/dilorenzo40.html.

Dobie, J. Frank. *The Flavor of Texas.* Austin: Jenkins Publishing Company, 1975.

Downing, Charles G., and Roy L. Swift. "Howard, Richard Austin." *New Handbook of Texas,* 3: 744–745. Austin: Texas State Historical Association, 1996.

BIBLIOGRAPHY

Duff, Kathryn, with Betty Kay Seibt. *Catclaw Country: An Informal History of Abilene in West Texas.* Burnet: Eakin Press, 1980.

Dumble, E. T. "Physical Geography, Geology, and Resources." *A Comprehensive History of Texas* II (1845–1897). Austin: Texas State Historical Association/Center for Studies in Texas History, University of Texas, 1986 [Reprint].

Elkins, Emma Johnson. "Old Fort Phantom and Its Tragedies." *Hunter's Magazine* 1911, 21.

Elkins, John M. *Indian Fighting on the Texas Frontier.* Waco: Texian Press, 1929.

Ely, Glen Sample. "Bedlam at Belknap: Frontier Lawlessness on the Butterfield Overland Mail Road in Texas, 1858–1861." *West Texas Historical Association Year Book* 82 (2006), 81–101.

Ely, Glen Sample. "Gone From Texas and Trading with the Enemy: New Perspectives on Civil War in West Texas." *Southwestern Historical Quarterly* vol. 110, no. 4 (April 2007), 439–463.

Fagan, Brian M. *The Great Journey.* London: Thames and Hudson, Ltd., 1987.

Fain, Anna Kilpatrick. "Fort Phantom Hill." *The Houston Chronicle Rotogravure Magazine,* 1956, 129–152,

Fehrenbach, T. R. *Comanches: The Destruction of a People.* New York: Da Capo Press, 1974.

Fehrenbach, T. R. *Lone Star: A History of Texas and the Texans.* New York: American Legacy Press, 1968.

Fiedel, Stuart J. *Prehistory of the Americas.* Cambridge: Cambridge University Press, 1987.

Foreman, Carolyn Thomas. "General William Goldsmith Belknap." *Chronicles of Oklahoma* vol. 22, no. 2 (June 1942), 124.

"Fort Belknap Souvenir Plate. Notes and Documents." *The Chronicles of Oklahoma* 28, (1950), 206–212.

Fort Phantom Foundation. Brochure. Abilene, Texas

"Fort Smith, Gateway to the California Gold Fields." *The Arkansas News.* Spring 1996.

Foster, L. L. *Forgotten Texas Census.* Austin: Texas State Historical Association, 2001.

Fox, Daniel E. *Traces of Texas History: Archaeological Evidence of the Past 450 Years.* San Antonio: Corona Publishing Co., 1983.

Frantz, Joe B. "Notes and Documents: The Significance of Frontier Forts to Texas." *Southwestern Historical Quarterly* vol. 72, no. 2 (October, 1970), 204–205.

Frazier, Donald S. *Blood and Treasure.* College Station: Texas A&M Press, 1995.

Frazier, Donald S. "Johnson, Middleton Tate." *New Handbook of Texas,* 3: 959–960. Austin: Texas State Historical Association, 1996.

Freeman, Martha Doty. *A History of Fort Phantom Hill, The Post on the Clear Fork of the Brazos River, Jones County, Texas.* Abilene, Texas: The Fort Phantom Foundation, 1999.

Freeman, W. G. "Report of Inspection of 8th Military Department Made by Brevet Lt. Col. W.G. Freeman, Asst. Adjutant Gen. Pursuant to Instructions from Head Quarters of Army, April 22, 1853." M. L. Crimmins Papers, Briscoe Center for American History, University of Texas, Austin.

BIBLIOGRAPHY

G. W. Hill to Robert Neighbors, Fort Belknap, Texas, February 12, 1855. Box 2R275, Briscoe Center for American History, University of Texas, Austin.

Gallaway, B. P. "History in West Texas." *West Texas Historical Association Year Book* 48 (1972), 165–166.

Gard, Wayne. "The Mooar Brothers, Buffalo Hunters." *The Southwestern Historical Quarterly* vol. 63, no. 1 (July 1959), 31–45.

Gesick, E. John, Jr., and Bill Wright. *The Texas Kickapoo: Keepers of Tradition*. El Paso: University of Texas at El Paso, 1996.

Gibson, George, Washington, D.C., to General T. S. Jesup, Washington, D.C., March 18, 1853: Box No. 342, Entry 225, RG92. National Archives.

Gillentine, Captain N. W., Erath County, to Colonel J. B. Barry, December 9, 1864. James Buckner Barry Papers, Box 2B44. Briscoe Center for American History, University of Texas, Austin.

Goodnight, Charles, Goodnight, Texas to J. M. Sibley, Abilene, Texas, April 2, 1924. Goodnight Archive, Hardin-Simmons University Richardson Library, Abilene, Texas.

Grace, Hybernia. "The First Trip West on the Butterfield Stage." *West Texas Historical Association Year Book* 7 (June 1932), 62–74.

Grace, Hybernia. "Historical Sketch of Jones County." *West Texas Historical Association Year Book* 3 (1927), 30–40.

Graham, Roy Eugene. "Federal Fort Architecture in Texas during the Nineteenth Century." *Southwestern Historical Quarterly* vol. 74, no. 2 (October 1970), 165–188.

Grant, Bruce. *American Forts, Yesterday and Today*. New York: E. P. Dutton & Co., 1965.

Greene, A. C. *900 Miles on the Butterfield Trail*. Denton: University of North Texas Press, 1994.

Greene, A. C. *The Last Captive*. Austin: Encino Press, 1972.

Gwynne, S. C. *Empire of the Summer Moon: Quanah Parker and the Rise and Falll of the Comanches, the Most Powerful Indian Tribe in American History*. New York: Scribner, 2010.

Haley, J. Evetts. *Fort Concho and the Texas Frontier*. San Angelo, Texas: San Angelo Standard-Times, 1952.

Haley, J. Evetts. *Charles Goodnight: Cowman and Plainsman*. Norman: University of Oklahoma Press, 1949.

Harney, Colonel William S., San Antonio, Texas, to Brevet Major General R. Jones, Adjutant General, Washington D.C., April 1, 1851. Letters Received, 1851 [A-H], Box No. 5, Entry 5572, Part I, RG393. National Archives,

Hatcher, John. "Fort Phantom Hill." *Texas Military History* vol. 3, no. 3 (October 1941), 159–163.

Hatley, Allen G. *Bringing the Law to Texas: Crime and Violence in Nineteenth Century Texas*. LaGrange, TX: Centex Press, 2002.

Havins, T. R. "Activities of Company E, Frontier Battalion, Texas Rangers 1874–1880." *West Texas Historical Association Year Book* 11 (1935), 62–72.

Hoffman, David, Austin, Texas, to Curtis Tunnell, Austin, Texas, September 16, 1977. Copy in files of Rick Weatherl, Abilene, Texas.

BIBLIOGRAPHY

Holden, Frances Mayhugh. *Lambshead Before Interwoven: A Texas Range Chronicle 1848-1878*. College Station: Texas A&M University Press, 1982.

Holden, W. C. "Frontier Defense, 1846–1860." *West Texas Historical Association Year Book* 6 (1930), 39–71.

Holeman, David, comp. *Letters of Hard Times in Texas 1840–1890*. Austin: Roger Beacham, 1974.

Hollon, Eugene W. *Beyond the Cross Timbers: The Travels of Randolph B. Marcy*. Norman: University of Oklahoma Press, 1955.

Holmes, Floyd J. *Indian Fights on the Texas Frontier*. Fort Worth: Pioneer Publishing Company, 1927.

Houston, Virginia H. Taylor. "Surveying in Texas." *Southwestern Historical Quarterly* vol. 65, no. 2 (October 1961), 204–233.

Huddleston, Lee Eldridge. *Origins of the American Indians: European Concepts, 1492–1729*. Austin: University of Texas Press, 1967.

Hudson, Linda S. *Mistress of Manifest Destiny: A Biography of Jane McManus Storm Cazneau 1807–1878*. Austin: Texas State Historical Association, 2001.

Hughes, John Taylor. *Doniphan's Expedition*. Chicago: Rio Grande Press, 1962.

Hunt, Colonel Thomas F., New Orleans, Louisiana, to Major General Thomas S. Jesup, Washington, D.C., December 22, 1852. Box No. 799, Entry 225, RG92. National Archives.

Hunt, Colonel Thomas F., New Orleans, Louisiana, to Major George W. F. Wood, Preston, Texas, December 21, 1852. Box No. 799, Entry 225, RG92. National Archives.

Hunt, James Winford. *Buffalo Days: Stories from J. Wright Mooar.* edited by Robert F. Pace Abilene, TX: State House Press, 2005.

Hutto, Homer, and Hooper Shelton. *Jones Country, Texas: The First 100 Years*. Stamford, TX: Shelton Press, 1978.

Jackson, Jack. *Imaginary Kingdom: Texas as Seen by the Rivera and Rubi Military Expeditions 1727 and 1767*. Austin: Texas State Historical Association, 1995.

Jacobson, Lucy Miller, and Mildred Bloys Nored. *Jeff Davis County, Texas*. Fort Davis, TX: Fort Davis Historical Society, 1993.

Jenkins, John H., and Kenneth Kesselus. *Edward Burleson: Texas Frontier Leader*. Austin: Jenkins, 1990.

Jones, Adjutant General R., Washington, D.C., to Brevet Brigadier General W. K. Belknap, July 2, 1851. Letters Received, 1851 [A-H], Box No. 5, Entry 5572, Part I, RG393. National Archives.

Jones, Adjutant General R., Washington, D.C., to Brevet Brigadier General M. Arbuckle, Fort Smith, Arkansas, June 14, 1851. Letters Received, 1851 [A-H], Box No. 5, Part I, Entry 5572, RG393. National Archives.

Jones, Mrs. J. Lee, and Richardson, Rupert N. "Colorado City, the Cattlemen's Capital." *West Texas Historical Association Year Book*, 19 (1943), 36–63.

Kemp, L. W. "Kerr, Peter." *New Handbook of Texas* 3:1076–1077. Austin: Texas State Historical Association, 1996.

Kincaid, Naomi Hatton, "The Abilene Reporter News and Its Contribution to the Building of the Abilene Country." Master's thesis, Hardin-Simmons University, Abilene, TX, 1945.

Kingston, Mike. "A Brief Sketch of Texas History." In: *Texas Almanac 2004–2005* Dallas: The Dallas Morning News, 2004, 31–55.

Koch, Lena Clara. "The Federal Indian Policy in Texas, 1845–1860." *Southwestern Historical Quarterly* vol. 28, no. 3 (January 1925), 223–234.

Koch, Lena Clara. "The Federal Indian Policy in Texas, 1845–1860." *Southwestern Historical Quarterly* vol. 28, no. 4 (April 1925), 257–286.

Landers, Emmett M. "A Short History of Taylor County." Master's thesis, Simmons University, Abilene, Texas, 1929.

Lang, Walter B. *The First Overland Mail: Butterfield Trail, St. Louis to San Francisco 1858–1861.* New York: Roycrofters, 1940.

Langellier, John P. *Army Blue: The Uniform of Uncle Sam's Regulars 1848–1873.* Atglen, PA: Schiffer Military History, 1998.

Leckie, William H. *The Buffalo Soldiers A Narrative of the Negro Calvary in the West.* Norman: University of Oklahoma Press, 1967.

Ledbetter, Barbara A. Neal. *Fort Belknap, Frontier Saga: Indians, Negroes and Anglo-Americans on the Texas Frontier.* Burnet, Texas: Eakin Press, 1982.

Ledbetter, Barbara A. Neal. *The Fort Belknap of Yesterday and Today 1851–1963.* Newcastle, Texas: n.p., 1963.

Lewis, Kenneth E., and Martha Royce Blaine. *Fort Washita, From Past to Present: An Archaeological Report.* Oklahoma Historical Society Series in Anthropology, Number 1: Kenneth E. Lewis, ed., 1975.

Lewis, Second Lieutenant W. H., Post on the Clear Fork of the Brazos, Texas, to Colonel S. Cooper, Washington D.C. December 5 1852. Roll 466, M-567. National Archives.

Lynch, Vernon. "Fort Griffin (Shackleford County)." *The Handbook of Texas,* 2:1102. Austin: Texas State Historical Association, 1996.

Mallory, W. M. *Treaties, Conventions, International Acts, Protocols, and Agreements.* Washington, D.C.: U.S. Government Printing Office, 1913.

Maltby, William J. *Captain Jeff or Frontier Life in Texas with the Texas Rangers.* Waco: Texian Press, 1967.

Mansfield, Joseph K. F. *Mansfield on the Condition of Western Forts 1853–1854.* Norman: University of Oklahoma Press, 1963.

Marcy, Captain R. B. "Report of Captain R. B. Marcy on His Exploration of Indian Territory and Northwest Texas." *West Texas Historical Year Book* 14 (1938), 116–136.

"Marcy, Randolph Barnes (1812–1887)," *Encyclopedia of Oklahoma History and Culture.* Accessed September 19, 2012, at http://digital.library.okstate.edu /encyclopedia/entries/M/MA021.html.

Marcy, R. B. *Thirty Years of Army Life on the Border.* New York: Harper and Brothers, 1866.

Marler, Charles H. "The Prophet from Abilene." *West Texas Historical Association Yearbook* 48 (1972), 37–62.

BIBLIOGRAPHY

Matthews, Sallie Reynolds. *Interwoven: A Pioneer Chronicle.* El Paso: C. Hertzog, 1958.

Mawson, Donald D. "The Federal Military Defense of the Northwest Texas Frontier, 1846–1861." Master's thesis, Hardin-Simmons University, Abilene, TX, 1971.

McCombs, Joe S. "On the Cattle Trail, and Buffalo Range." *West Texas Historical Association Year Book* 11 (1935), 93–101.

McConnell, Joseph. *The West Texas Frontier: A Descriptive History of Early Times in Western Texas.* Jacksboro, Texas: Gazette Print, 1933.

McLaurine, W. C., Dallas, Texas, to Jim Dan Hill, Abilene, Texas, November 15, 1972. Vertical File "Fort Phantom Hill," Richardson Research Center, Hardin-Simmons University, Abilene, Texas.

McLean, Malcolm D. "Robertson, Elijah Sterling Clack." *The New Handbook of Texas,* 5: 615–616. Austin: Texas State Historical Association, 1996.

Mears, Mildred Watkins. "The Three Forts in Coryell County." *Southwestern Historical Quarterly* vol. 67, no. 1 (July 1963), 1–14.

Merchant, C. L. Interview by John Crutchfield, March 26 1923. Carl Coke Rister Collection, Southwest Collection, Texas Tech University, Lubbock, Texas.

Miles, Brevet Lieutenant Colonel D. S., Fort Washita, Cherokee Nation, to Quartermaster General Major General Thomas S. Jesup, Washington City, January 3, 1850. Box No. 1217, Entry 225, RG92. National Archives.

Moore, Stephen L. *Taming Texas: Captain William T. Sadler's Lone Star Service.* Austin: State House Press, 2000.

Myers, John. *The Westerners.* Lincoln: University of Nebraska Press, 1969.

Myres, Sandra L. "Fort Graham: Listening Post on the Texas Frontier." *West Texas Historical Association Year Book* 59 (1983), 33–51.

Newcomb, Samuel P. *The Diary of Samuel P. Newcomb: January 1, 1865 to December 21, 1865.* Abilene, Texas: private printing, 1865.

O'Neal, Ben G. "The Beginnings of Fort Belknap." *Southwestern Historical Quarterly* vol. 61, no. 4 (April 1958). 508–521.

Ormsby, W. L. *The Butterfield Overland Mail.* edited by L. H. Wright and J. M. Bynum. San Marino, California: Huntington Library, 1954.

Pace, Robert F., and Donald S. Frazier. *Frontier Texas: History of a Borderland to 1880.* Abilene, Texas: State House Press, 2004.

Pool, William C. "The Battle of Dove Creek." *Southwestern Historical Quarterly* vol. 53, no. 4 (April 1950), 367–385.

Pool, William C., ed. "Westward I Go Free: The Memoirs of William E. Cureton, Texas Frontiersman." *Southwestern Historical Quarterly* vol. 81, no. 2 (October 1977), 155–190.

Pool, William C., and Edward Triggs. *A Historical Atlas of Texas.* Austin: Encino Press, 1975.

Ramos, Mary G. "Camp Cooper, Fort Belknap, and the Indian Reservations." In: *Texas Almanac 2004–2005,* 26. Dallas: The Dallas Morning News, 2003.

Ramos, Mary. "Women at the Frontier Forts." In: *Texas Almanac 2004–2005,* 22–25. Dallas: The Dallas Morning News, 2003.

Reid, Stuart. *The Secret War for Texas.* College Station: Texas A&M University Press, 2007.

Richardson, Albert D. *Beyond the Mississippi: From the Great River to the Great Ocean: Life and Adventure on the Prairies, Mountains, and Pacific Coast.* Hartford, CT: American Publishing Company, 1867.

Richardson, Rupert N. *Along Texas Old Forts Trail.* Abilene, TX: Nel Fry, 1972.

Richardson, Rupert N. "Jim Shaw, the Delaware." *West Texas Historical Yearbook* 3 (1927), 3–12.

Richardson, Rupert N. *The Comanche Barrier to South Plains Settlement.* Abilene, TX: Hardin-Simmons University, 1991, 44

Richardson, Rupert N. *The Frontier of Northwest Texas, 1846–1876: Advance and Defense by the Pioneer Settlers of the Cross Timbers and Prairies.* Glendale, CA: Arthur H. Clark Company, 1963.

Richardson, Rupert N., ed. "Documents Relating to West Texas and Its Indian Tribes." *West Texas Historical Association Yearbook* (1925), 34.

Richardson, Rupert N., ed., "Marcy's Reconnaissance through Northern and Western Texas." *West Texas Historical Yearbook* 1 (1925), 32–53.

Richardson, T. C. 1997. "Goodnight-Loving Trail." *New Handbook of Texas* 3: 244–245. Austin: Texas State Historical Association, 1996.

Rister, C. C. "Fort Phantom and Its Military History." *Frontier Times* (December 1925), 36–40.

Rister, Carl C. and Rupert N. Richardson, Buffalo Gap, Texas, to Mr. Scott, March 25, 1923. C. C. Rister Papers, Box 10. Southwest Collection, Texas Tech University, Lubbock, Texas.

Rister, Carl Coke. *Fort Griffin on the Texas Frontier.* Norman: University of Oklahoma Press, 1956.

Rister, Carl Coke. "Fort Phantom Hill and Its Military History." *The Western Weekly,* October 4, 1925.

Rister, Carl Coke. *Robert E. Lee in Texas.* Norman: University of Oklahoma Press, 1946.

Rister, Carl Coke. "The Border Post of Fort Phantom Hill." *West Texas Historical Association Year Book* 14 (1938), 3–13.

Rister, Carl Coke. *The Southwestern Frontier—1865–1881.* Cleveland: The Arthur H. Clark Company, 1928.

Roberts, Laura G., Nugent, Texas, to Mrs. Frank Huie, February 23, 1936. Jones County, Texas, Collection, 1881–1961. Southwest Collection, Texas Tech University, Lubbock, Texas.

Robinson, Charles III. *The Frontier World of Fort Griffin: The Life and Death of a Western Town.* Western Lands and Water Series 17. Spokane, Washington: The Arthur H. Clark Company, 1992.

"Santanta and Big Tree." *Fort Worth Democrat.* September 13, 1873.

Schmidly, David J. *Texas Natural History: A Century of Change.* Lubbock: Texas Tech University Press, 2002.

Scobee, Barry. *Fort Davis Texas 1583–1960.* Fort Davis, TX: Self-Published, 1963.

"Scotty Philip, the Man Who Saved the Buffalo," Philip Chamber of Commerce. Accessed October 1, 2012, at http://www.philipsouthdakota.com/other_7.html.

BIBLIOGRAPHY

Scurlock, Dan, Austin, Texas to National Archives, Washington D.C, April 6, 1971. Copy in files of Rick Weatherl, Abilene, Texas.

Scurlock, Dan, Austin, Texas, to Richard Dillard, Abilene, Texas, June 2, 1975. Copy in files of Rick Weatherl, Abilene, Texas.

Shirk, George H. "Mail Call at Fort Washita." *The Chronicles of Oklahoma* 3 (1955), 14–35.

Sibley, Brevet Major H.H., Fort Graham, Texas, to Department of Texas Headquarters, July 24, 1851. Volume 2, Entry 4776, RG393. National Archives.

Sibley, Captain C.C ., Post on Clear Fork of the Brazos River, Texas, to Honorable W. H. Bissett, Washington City, D.C., January 16, 1853. Roll 488, M-567. National Archives.

Sibley, Captain H. H., Post on Clear Fork Brazos River, to Major R. S. Neighbors, October 8, 1853. Bureau of Indian Affairs, Letters Received, 1846–1855, Box 2R275. Briscoe Center for American History, University of Texas, Austin.

Smith, David Paul. *Frontier Defense in the Civil War: Texas Rangers and Rebels*. College Station: Texas A&M University Press, 1992.

Smith, Brevet Major General Persifor F., San Antonio, Texas to Brevet Lieutenant Colonel W. W. J. Bliss, Western Division, September 28, 1851. Letters Received, 1851 (J-W and unentered), Box No. 6, Entry 5572, Part I, RG393. National Archives.

Smith, Brevet Major General Persifor F., San Antonio, Texas, to Governor P. H. Bell, August 9, 1852. Part 1, Entry 5572, RG393. National Archives.

Smith, Brevet Major General Persifor F., San Antonio, Texas, to Brevet Lieutenant Colonel W. W. J. Bliss, Western Division, May 9, 1852. Letters Received, 1852 [A-L], Box No. 7, Entry 5572, Part I, RG393. National Archives.

Smith, Brevet Major General Persifor F., San Antonio, Texas, to Brevet Lieutenant Colonel W. W. J. Bliss, Western Division, March 22, 1852. Roll 471, M-567. National Archives.

Smith, Persifor F. Brevet Maj. General, Camp of 5th Infantry on the Salt Fork of the Brazos, to Brevet Lieutenant Colonel W. W. J. Bliss, Western Division, November 3, 1851. Letters Received, 1851 (J-W and unentered), Box No. 6, Entry 5572, Part I, RG393. National Archives.

Smith, Ralph A. "Old West Texas Limekilns Are Mostly Mysteries, Memories, and Material Remains." *West Texas Historical Association Year Book* 52 (1976), 16–37.

Stanton, Assistant Quarter Master General Henry, St. Louis, Missouri, to Major General T. S. Jesup, Washington, D.C., June 12, 1851: Box 132, Entry 225, NM-81, RG92. National Archives.

Steinert, Wilhelm. *North America, Particularly Texas In the Year 1849: A Travel Account*. Dallas: DeGolyer Library & William P. Clements Center for Southwest Studies, 2005.

Stevenson, Captain C. L., Camp Belknap, Brazos, Texas, to Major General R. Jones, Washington, D.C., September 1, 1851. Roll 441, M-567. National Archives.

Swift, Roy L. "Chihuahua Expedition." *New Handbook of Texas* 2: 76–77. Austin: Texas State Historical Association, 2006.

Taylor, Travis. "Garrison Life at Fort Chadbourne, 1852–1861." *West Texas Historical Association Yearbook.* 87 (2011), 23–34.

Texas Bureau of Immigration. Texas, the Home for the Emigrant, from Everywhere/ Published by Authority of the Legislature and Under the Auspices of the Superintendent of Immigration of the State of Texas. Houston: A. C. Gray, 1875, The Portal to Texas History. Accessed May 6, 2013, at http://texashistory.unt.edu/data /UTA/meta-pth-28586.tkl.

Thian, Raphael P., Compiler. *Notes Illustrating the Military Geography of the United States*. Washington, D.C.: Government Printing Office, 1881.

Tompkins, Deputy Quarterly Master General D. D., San Antonio, Texas, to Major General T. S. Jesup, Washington, D.C.: Box No. 1139, Entry 225, RG92. National Archives.

Tunnell, Curtis, Austin, Texas, to Jim Alexander, Abilene, Texas, July 12, 1971. Copy in files of Rick Weatherl, Abilene, Texas.

US Bureau of Indian Affairs. *Annual Report of the Commissioner of Indian Affairs, 1854*. Washington, D.C.: Author, 1855.

Utley, Robert M. *Frontiersmen in Blue: The United States Army and the Indian, 1848–1865*. New York: Macmillan Company, 1967.

Utley, Robert M. *The Indian Frontier 1846–1890*. Albuquerque: University of New Mexico Press, 1984.

Van Cleef, June, and Bill Wright. *The Texas Outback: Ranching on the Last Frontier*. College Station: Texas A&M University Press, 2005.

Waite, Brevet Colonel C. A., Clear Fork of Brazos, to Department of Texas Headquarters, July 7, 1852. Volume 2, Entry 4776, RG393. National Archives.

Wallace, Edward S. "General William Jenkins Worth and Texas." *Southwestern Historical Quarterly* vol. 54, no. 2 (October 1950), 159–168.

Wallace, Ernest, and E. A. Hoebel. *The Comanches: Lords of the South Plains*. Norman: University of Oklahoma Press, 1952.

Wallace, Ernest, ed. "History in West Texas: Fort Phantom and the Old Forts Trail." *West Texas Historical Association Yearbook* 48 (1972), 165–166.

Wallace, Ernest, ed. *Ranald S. Mackenzie's Official Correspondence Relating to Texas, 1871–1873*. Lubbock: West Texas Museum Association, 1967.

Webb, Walter Prescott. *The Texas Rangers: A Century of Frontier Defense*, 2nd ed. Austin: University of Texas Press, 1965.

Wetteman, Jr., Robert P. "Siege of Fort Texas." In: *The United States and Mexico at War: Nineteenth-Century Expansionism and Conflict*, 162. New York: Simon and Schuster Macmillan, 1998.

Williams, J. W. "Marcy's Road from Dona Ana." *West Texas Historical Association Year Book* 19 (October 1943), 129–152.

Williams, J. W. "The Butterfield Overland Mail Road Across Texas." *Southwestern Historical Quarterly* vol. 61, no. 1 (July 1957), 1–19.

Williams, J.W. "The Marcy and the Butterfield Trails across North Texas." Unpublished Master's Thesis. Hardin-Simmons University, Abilene, Texas, 1938.

Williams, J. W. "Military Roads of the 1850's in Central West Texas." *West Texas Historical Association Year Book.* 18 (1942), 77–91.

BIBLIOGRAPHY

Wisconsin, The State Historical Society of. *A Guide to the Military Posts of the United States, 1789–1895*. Madison: Author, 1964.

Woolley, Bryan. *Texas Almanac 2004–2005*. Dallas: The Dallas Morning News, 2004.

Wooster, Robert. "Fort Davis and the Close of a Military Frontier." *Southwestern Historical Quarterly* vol. 110, no. 2 (October 2006), 173–192.

Wooster, Robert. "Military Strategy in the Southwest 1848–1860." *Military History of Texas and the Southwest* vol. 15, no. 1 (1979), 4–16.

Wooster, Robert. *Soldiers, Sutlers, and Settlers*. College Station: Texas A&M University Press, 1987.

Wright, Bill. "Fort Phantom Hill: The Misplaced Post on the Clear Fork of the Brazos." *Heritage* vol. 7, no. 3 (Summer 1997), 19–21.

Wright, John, & William. *Recollections of Western Texas. Descriptive and Narrative Including an Indian Campaign, 1852–1855*. Lubbock: Texas Tech University Press, 2001.

Yale University, Class of 1850. *Biographical Record of the Class of 1850, Yale College*. New Haven, CT: Tuttle, Morehouse & Taylor, Printer, 1877.

Zachry, Juanita Daniel. *A History of Rural Taylor County*. Austin, Texas: Eakin Press, 1980.

Index

INDEX

CPSIA information can be obtained at www.ICGtesting.com
Printed in the USA
LVOW06s0343220314

378379LV00004B/9/P